Closet
Monsters

Closet

Monsters

Stitch Creatures You'll Love from Clothing You Don't

written &
illustrated
by JOHN
MURPHY

LARK
CRAFTS

A Division of Sterling Publishing Co., Inc.
New York / London

SENIOR EDITOR: Terry Taylor

ART DIRECTOR: Kristi Pfeffer

ART PRODUCTION: 828, Inc.

PHOTOGRAPHER: Steve Mann

COVER DESIGNER: Kristi Pfeffer

Library of Congress Cataloging-in-Publication Data

Murphy, John (John C.), 1975-
  Closet monsters : stitch creatures you'll love from clothing you don't / John Murphy. -- 1st ed.
    p. cm.
  Includes index.
  ISBN 978-1-60059-604-9 (pb-trade pbk. : alk. paper)
  1. Textile crafts. 2. Recycling (Waste, etc.) I. Title.
TT699.M84 2010
 746--dc22

                           2010001545

10 9 8 7 6 5 4 3 2 1

First Edition

Published by Lark Books, A Division of
Sterling Publishing Co., Inc.
387 Park Avenue South, New York, NY 10016

Text © 2010, John Murphy
Photography © 2010, Lark Books, A Division of Sterling Publishing Co., Inc.
Illustrations © 2010, John Murphy

Distributed in Canada by Sterling Publishing,
c/o Canadian Manda Group, 165 Dufferin Street
Toronto, Ontario, Canada M6K 3H6

Distributed in the United Kingdom by GMC Distribution Services,
Castle Place, 166 High Street, Lewes, East Sussex, England BN7 1XU

Distributed in Australia by Capricorn Link (Australia) Pty Ltd.,
P.O. Box 704, Windsor, NSW 2756 Australia

If you have questions or comments about this book, please contact:
Lark Books
67 Broadway
Asheville, NC 28801
828-253-0467

Manufactured in China

ISBN 13: 978-1-60059-604-9

For information about custom editions, special sales, premium and corporate purchases, please contact Sterling Special Sales Department at 800-805-5489 or specialsales@sterlingpub.com.

For information about desk and examination copies available to college and university professors, requests must be submitted to academic@larkbooks.com. Our complete policy can be found at www.larkbooks.com.

Contents!

6   Introduction

8   Closet Monster Basics

8   You Gotta Have Clothes!
9   Fabric Is Awesome
11   Basic Sewing Supplies
13   The Zen of Disassembly & Stitching
18   Closet Monster Anatomy

34   Meet the Monsters

36   **Flapp & Cuff**
44   **Lurwin Obsgarde**
52   **Wazman Standers**
62   **Gilmor & Ronny Oothby**
72   **Ulee Bingham**
80   **Camilla Grace**
88   **Maureen McDoover**
96   **The Mighty Glapthod**
102   **Zazmyrna Hoag**
110   **Julian Van Voon**
118   **Blarty Dween**
126   **BooFaye Bovelle Bernadella**
134   **Precious Mumpkins**

142   About the Author
142   Acknowledgments
143   Index

This book is dedicated to Ian, Paden, Craig, and Amaka.

Introduction

{ *I've received countless letters and photos from crafters all over the world about their adventures with my first book, Stupid Sock Creatures. I don't want my readers to abandon their love for socks, but it's time for the next step in creature evolution.* }

We humans love to manufacture and buy "stuff," and for decades our habit has been to throw away anything we no longer wanted. We're changing that mindset quite rapidly as people all over the world have discovered a gold mine of raw material for creativity and reuse. I want to encourage your aptitude for resourcefulness and creativity with whatever you have around you—especially what is in your closet.

You know your closet contains garments that you no longer wear—they don't fit, they're out of style, or they're just forgotten. You can hope they come back in style in your lifetime, but they probably won't fit when they do! So, let's discover their hidden potential for monster making and perform massive reconstructive surgery on them to bring to life your own Closet Monster.

I want you to use this book as a springboard for your own creativity. As with socks, certain parts and certain aspects of more complex garments lend themselves to monster body parts. The instructions in this book will help you see the monster potential in each panel and section of a garment as you disassemble it.

I didn't use garments from my closet for the monsters in this book—there isn't a muumuu or skirt in there. I chose common, universal garments that everyone may have in their closet. If you don't have a buffalo plaid jacket for making Lurwin Obsgarde (page 44), you don't need to run out and buy a new one. Use an old jacket you already have, and follow any instructions within this book that apply. I used a stretchy, loudly printed house dress to make Zazmyrna Hoag (page 102), but you could use a bridesmaid's dress, graduation robe, or an old curtain (just like a certain southern belle). And even if you have a dusty rose blazer, as used in Julian Van Voon's project (page 110), your blazer might yield different parts when disassembled. That's not a problem. If you're too attached to every item in your closet, get out of the house and go shopping at second-hand shops or your local charity store. You might even find the same dress that Zazmyrna wears. It's a scary thought, but true.

The patterns and instructions in this book are, essentially, suggestions. I'll show detailed disassemblies for the garments featured. Once you see how a garment is broken down into its basic shapes, you'll begin to see those shapes as monster parts. Often, very little alteration is needed for those parts to come to life. You'll repurpose them as arms, legs, bodies, or horns just as they are. Of course, it's perfectly fine to whack those pieces into shapes you want as well! That's done a lot of times in this book as well.

Have fun with this book and create your own community of Closet Monsters. Learn my tricks of the trade from the basics and then use what you've learned to create one of my projects and then one of your own! Reuse and repurposing are the creative keys to unlock unlimited possibilities. So purge your closets and let's get started.

Pay attention, fleshlings!

{ *Stupid Sock Creatures—my first book—was a great beginner text for plush crafters: socks are easy to stitch by hand. Closet Monsters are just a bit more complex, so I stitched all of them using a sewing machine. I recommend that you use a sewing machine, too—it's a time saver and makes stitching multiple layers so much easier. That said, let's talk about the stuff you'll need to craft your very own closet monster.* }

You Gotta Have Clothes!

First and absolutely foremost, you're going to need all kinds of clothes to massacre. Shut your eyes for a moment and picture the clothes stored away in the deepest recesses of your closet. Have you not worn them in half a decade? Are they ugly? Do you see any of the following items?

Trousers, slacks, knickers, pants, and shorts
Suits and blazers for men and ladies
Skirts, dresses, gowns, cocktail dresses, and muumuus
Overcoats, windbreakers, jackets, and raincoats
Dress shirts, blouses, and t-shirts
Pajamas, nighties, and robes
Sweatshirts, sweatpants, yoga pants, and track suits
Sweaters and vests

If your own closet is lacking all of these items, just what do you wear? Have no fear: thrift and charity shops have every imaginable kind of garment you could need to create closet monsters and more. It's OK to buy something for a monster if your own closet is bare. Charity shops not only need your donations, they also need your financial support.

You can go door-to-door in your neighborhood and introduce yourself as a local crafter with a willingness to take burdensome items of clothing off people's hands. Unless you know someone very well, though, don't ask if you can look in his or her closet. That's a sure way to get a door slammed in your face or worse. In many cases, people who can't be bothered to go to a charity drop-off will be glad to give you their unwanted clothes.

If you want something specific, you may have to search high and low for that perfect cashmere jacket or faux Chanel suit. But it can be done! Online auction sites and high-end consignment shops may be where you need to look.

No matter where you find an article of clothing you want to bring to life as a monster, launder or dry clean the item before you disassemble it. Every monster deserves a fresh and clean beginning.

In this book, you'll learn the techniques, methods, and procedures for making closet monsters, as opposed to copying precise patterns. What fun would that be? It's not likely that you'll be able to find an exact duplicate of the ugly pink blazer I used to make Julian Van Voon (page 110) or the muumuu that produced Zazmyrna Hoag (page 102). Teaching you techniques rather than giving you precise patterns will enable you to find potential in whatever you have at hand. I hope you'll apply your own creativity and go beyond these instructions. I also hope you'll send me photos of the creatures you make to www.stupidcreatures.com.

Full disclosure: I didn't ravage my own closet to make the creatures in this book. I've never owned a muumuu! I chose the types of garments almost everyone has hanging in their closet. You may not have a plaid wool coat or an acid green skirt suit, but you will undoubtedly have something similar or even better than what I used.

Fabric is Awesome

Any garment is suitable for the projects in this book—even leather chaps if you're so inclined (though leather is tricky to sew). Before you disassemble your clothes, read the labels. Knowing what your fabric is made of will help you know how to clean it when your monster goes on a messy food binge, what kind of needle and thread to use, what sort of other fabrics it can be attached to, how it might be ironed, or whether it will fray when cut.

Durable, exterior fabric most likely can be used for the main parts of your creature. Silky or slinky lining fabric is best suited for appliqué and other non-structural parts such as the ear lining or the inside of a mouth.

If you plan on combining different fabrics into one monster, make sure the fabrics are similar enough in weight, thickness, and stretch (if applicable) to be sewn together and stuffed. For instance, denim and knit fabrics are too dissimilar to stitch together: their attachment could rupture at the seam when stuffed or handled.

Here's a quick reference for the kinds of fabrics we'll be using in the book and how they behave when being made into stuffed monsters.

Cotton shirting cuts easily, doesn't readily fray, and isn't stretchy. Basic geometric shapes work well with cotton.

Woven wool should be cut carefully in single layers; it slides a bit when layered and cut together. It's usually thick, so do what you can to avoid having to sew through too many layers (more than two) at a time. Use wool for larger, simpler shaped creatures: its thickness will make turning out and stuffing small, tight, or complex shapes very difficult.

Knit wool sweaters are wonderful, if somewhat problematic to work with: they fray like mad and can be difficult to sew.

Laa!

If you're buying a sweater to use, look for one that's already shrunken: you'll notice that right away. If you purchase a wool sweater in fine condition, you can felt it before you start your project. Disregard the label and wash it in hot water, then tumble dry on high heat. Now you can cut it without too much fraying. I use a zigzag stitch or wide overcast stitch when I sew with knit wool. Make larger rather than smaller creatures from sweater material because the thick seam allowance makes turning and stuffing a challenge.

Corduroy and **denim** are accommodating and sturdy. Both fabrics are deceptively pliant, so you can make large or small creatures with them. Multiple layers of these fabrics can be both machine and hand sewn. Use the wrong side of the fabric to create a second tone or texture on the outside. You'll make some incredible monsters with these materials. Stuff them as firmly as you like. This fabric can take it.

Knits vary in thickness from tees to polo shirts and sweats. Raveling and fraying isn't much of a problem with knits, but thinner knits tend to roll up at the edge. This is easily remedied by pinning. Sometimes knits boast a dual texture, with a smooth outside and a pilled or fuzzy inside. If your knit fabric is on the thicker side, it can become challenging to sew through four or more layers. Most knits stretch just enough to handle curves and angles without compromising your seams when turned out and stuffed.

Flannel is an easy fabric to work with and it doesn't fray much. Straight lines and simple shapes always make good creature parts, but flannel can handle some adventurous curvy and angular variations. Stuff adequately, but not too firmly. Flannel has a grain (stretch direction) that needs to be observed. While I'm a bit cavalier about the grain, overstuffing can stress the seams where parts with opposing grains are attached.

Suitings and **tweeds** come with many different qualities, weights, and textures. This book features two projects using some of the ugliest, synthetic suiting fabrics this side of the grave. If it weren't for the glued masses of interfacing stuck to nearly every piece of those garments, I'm sure the fabric would have frayed wildly. The fabric cuts easily, but care must be taken when handling and sewing. Keep your shapes angular or mildly curved. Stuff thoroughly, but not too firmly.

Stretchy synthetics are sometimes cheaply made and their creepy texture has a propensity to snag on hangnails or whiskers. Other than that, these materials often feature a printed side and a blank side that you can use as two different tones. They cut without a problem owing to the miracle of science, so the edges don't fray! The fabric is strong enough to be stuffed as firmly as you like and it stretches. You can count on making chubby creatures with this stuff.

Um, I have a thing to do. See you on page 88.

Basic Sewing Supplies

The sewing supplies needed for these projects are probably universal to every sewer, so you might only need to pop out to the craft store for just a few things. I'll run through the list anyway just to be thorough.

You'll need a **sewing machine** with a straight stitch and a zigzag stitch at least. We'll be doing quite a bit of sewing on each monster, sometimes through thick fabrics like wool, denim, corduroy, and felt. A sewing machine will give you the speed and power that stitching with a thread and needle can't provide. We'll be using straight stitches most of the time, but zigzag and other overcast stitches will come in handy when doing appliqué and working with fabrics that stretch or are prone to fray.

You will also need **sewing machine needles** that were designed to fit your machine, and suit the fabrics you choose. Fabrics have different weaves, fiber content, and thicknesses, and thus require needles with the right point and width to go through them effectively. Needles are typically sold in packs of four or five. A fabric store clerk can help you choose the right needles for your machine and your project.

If you don't have a sewing machine, you will need the following items: sewing needles, thimbles, patience, and, perhaps, bandages.

Straight pins are very important. I use long, sturdy quilting pins with big, visible yellow heads. You can get these in packs of 250 or 500. They're not terribly cheap, but you'll use them again and again, and you won't be sad you bought them. I like long pins because their length makes them easier to grasp

and handle, and their big yellow heads make them visible. You need to be able to see your pins, otherwise you might forget about them and poke yourself when you handle your project. I am a big fan of pins and will do my best to show you when and where pinning is needed. You'll either see an image of a pin with a robust, visible head (as I strongly recommend you use), though to save any crowding of diagrammatic elements, the literal pin may be replaced with a small, thick X.

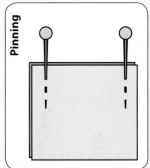

I use **polyester all-purpose thread** for general sewing because it's sturdier than cotton thread and can handle the rigors of moving quickly through a sewing machine.

Upholstery thread is smooth, sturdy, and much more resilient than polyester thread. I use it for hand-stitching tasks such as closing stuffing holes and attaching add-ons. This stuff is less prone to tangle when hand sewing than all-purpose thread.

Fusible adhesive webbing is an absolute must-have for appliqué (see page 33). It's used to bond appliqué pattern pieces to the background fabric. Fusibles can be purchased by the yard, in 1-yard (.91 m) packages, or in rolls. Most can be sewn, but others can't, and will gum-up your sewing machine needle. Check the material you purchase!

Measuring and Marking

Use a **24-inch (61 cm) ruler or yardstick** for general measurement and as a straight edge for cutting your fabric. A **flexible ruler** is handy when you're measuring unusual curved lines.

I use a **curved, plastic, fashion ruler** to accurately calculate and measure curved lines for tracing and cutting. I use it for measuring round creature bottoms or the soles of feet, but you don't have to have one to make the creatures.

To trace shapes and make cutting marks on fabrics, use **fabric pens** or **tailor's chalk**. Most fabric pens use washable ink. Some come with ink that disappears. I sometimes cheat and use a ballpoint pen. Ballpoint ink doesn't bleed, and the marks are made on the wrong side of the fabric so they're forever concealed within the creature when it's stuffed and closed.

I am your RULER, pitiful mortals!

Fashion Ruler

Cutting and Disassembly

You will want good-quality, **sharp fabric scissors** as well as **scissors for cutting paper**. You mustn't cut paper with your fabric scissors because paper dulls the blades. Fabric scissors are just too much of an investment to treat so casually. Paper scissors will be used for cutting the fusible adhesive webbing we'll use for appliqué.

You'll want a **craft knife** with a #11 blade for popping seams. The blades tend to dull noticeably from this kind of work, so keep plenty of spare blades on hand.

And every sewer needs in his or her arsenal at least one **seam ripper** for picking at stubborn seams.

A **rotary cutter** and **self-healing, gridded cutting mat** are wonderful tools to add to your arsenal, but aren't absolutely necessary for these projects.

Stuffings and Fillers

Polyester fiberfill is sold in bags of various sizes at most craft and fabric stores. Ask your fabric store retailer if the store stocks recycled fiberfill. You may be surprised to find out that your favorite stuffing was made from recycled plastic bottles.

Stuffing reclaimed from old furniture, cleaned and repackaged into gigantic 30 lb (13.6 kg) bags is called **grade 2 fiberfill**. I like to use this fiberfill: it's coarser than new fiberfill, and tends to pack more densely. Plus, it's less expensive per pound than the new stuff, and it's easy on the environment.

Use **fabric scraps** to fill out the larger shapes of your creature. You'll save clean up time by entire seconds. The consummate recycler will use every tiny cutting of fabric to its utmost potential.

Polypropylene pellets (also known as beanbag fill) are standard for mass-marketed toys you find in stores. You can find them at craft and fabric stores in 8 oz (226 g) bags. Polypropylene is pricey, but it's infinitely recyclable. Other petroleum plastics can be recycled a few times but they disintegrate eventually. Polypropylene, for whatever reason (ask a chemist), maintains its structure over time and can be recycled again and again.

Flax seeds, **buckwheat groats**, or **mung beans** can be used instead of polypropylene pellets if you want to go au naturale! You can purchase them in bulk at health food stores. Flax seeds and buckwheat groats are tiny fillers that compact snugly in fingers and tails; mung beans are best used in larger spaces.

Pressing and Appliqué

You'll need an **iron** and an **ironing board** for these projects. Giving the parts of your disassembled garment a good pressing will make it easier to measure and cut the shapes you want. Ironing the seams after you stitch can give your project a crisp, professional look.

A **pressing cloth** is a piece of soft cotton fabric that creates a barrier between your fabric and a hot iron. It helps you iron sheer, delicate or synthetic fabrics without scorching them. If you don't have a pressing cloth, use a soft, cotton handkerchief or a big swatch of cotton jersey (t-shirt) material. In a pinch, you can even use clean paper from your printer.

I use a **fusible adhesive webbing** to attach appliqués to fabric. And I always use a pressing cloth when I'm ironing the appliqué webbing to delicate fabrics and to protect the iron from sticking on stray bits of webbing. You should, too, or your iron will be sorry.

Pieces of Wow

When your creature is finished, you may want to adorn it with decorative embellishments. Things that can be sewn, pinned, or tied onto your creature once it's finished can set off its finished look and give it character—use your fertile imagination! Here's a brief list of items you can use, aside from plain, old shirt buttons, hideous bows, and corporate logos:

Fancy buttons
Jingly bells
Belt buckles
Political or humorous pins and buttons
Orphaned earrings
Sparkly brooches
Soda can pull tabs
Patches from your old scouting uniform
Nametag pins
Washers, cogs, wingnuts
Coins from overseas
Bottle caps
Shoelaces

Do.

The Zen of Disassembly and Stitching

Before I make each creature, I have to cut apart an article of clothing or, as I like to refer to it, engage in some **disassembly**. When I disassemble a garment, I can see all of the fabric shapes that it yielded. Then, I look at the shapes objectively and re-imagine them as creature body parts rather than parts of clothes. A pants leg might become a body or very, very long legs. And a pocket is not always something you put things in. I've created **Disassembly Charts** for each project in this book. Take a look at one and see if you can recognize a creature of your own invention.

Before we discuss specific disassembly methods, we must talk about your mindset. You're not sitting down with lacy teddy bears and a cup of tea here. I mean, you can make tea if you want, but the mood here is anything but lacy and predictable. Don't worry about explaining yourself to anyone. You're making monsters, after all. Picture them creeping out of the closet. Feel them in the room with you. Just as Michelangelo saw a finished statue inside a block of marble, you should look for the living, breathing monster which justifies a terrible garment's disassembly in the first place. Go ahead: channel the monsters, and they'll reveal themselves to you as you work your wonders.

The whole point of this book hinges on this one very important step: for new monsters to be made, clothing must be disassembled! There are innovative ways to go about it. Using a lawnmower, weed whacker, or paper shredder makes short work of taking apart clothing. My favorite method is the CESS method (Close Eyes, Scream, and Stab). I'll now explain effective and more practical methods that you should actually use.

Re.

Mi.

Speak up! My hearing aid just died.

Cut the Seams

This method is easy: simply cut off all of the seams. Turn your clothing wrong side out, and then use **sharp fabric scissors** or a **rotary cutter** to cut right along the edges of the seam. This method is quick. It yields nice, flat pieces of fabric, shaped in ways that will inspire monster anatomy. And those thick, ropey seams you remove can be saved and used for monster parts such as hair or fingers.

Focus on the tip of the scissors when cutting, not the deepest depths of the fulcrum where you have less control. Aim and point the tip of your scissors exactly where you want them to go, and snip small, careful cuts.

If you use a rotary cutter, use a new, sharp blade. The blades are somewhat expensive, so take care of them. If you're using a rotary cutter against a straight edge, make sure the edge is plastic. Metal rulers, while durable, will dull the sharp edge of a rotary blade quickly.

Rip the Seams

This method is a bit more painstaking and a tad more time consuming. Cut the stitching of your seams with a seam ripper or a craft knife. Do this if you really wanted to be thrifty with your fabric harvesting, or to take advantage of the often interesting fold marks a seam leaves in your fabric. This method is best practiced of you have OCD tendencies or simply want to lose yourself in a meditative state of repetitive action.

If you've never used a seam ripper before here's what you do: insert the pointed tip of the **seam ripper** under one of the stitches. Pop the stitch. Continue using that pointed tip and edge to lift other stitches out from the seam until you have perhaps 1/2 inch (1.3 cm) of exposed thread. Move 1 inch (2.5 cm) or so down the seam and repeat the process. Pull the exposed thread at one end and tug the released length of thread out of the seam. Do this until the whole seam has been released. It's tedious, but satisfying.

Working with a **craft knife** is just as simple, and I think a bit neater. Pry the seam of your garment apart just enough to expose the first few stitches. Slice them apart with your blade. As you cut one stitch, you'll be able to gently pry the seam apart several stitches further. Do not rip or yank, even if you're tempted. If you're working out a deeply-rooted childhood pain, find something else to rip and yank. Anyway, continue carefully slicing stitches and prying the seam open until you've

cut it all and your fabrics are separated. Way easy.

Now that your clothing is disassembled, look at your pieces. You'll see that the fabric has a right and a wrong side. You can choose to use either side of the fabric, but the right side usually looks nicer than the wrong side.

In the diagrams in this book, the wrong side of the fabric will be indicated with the same color as its right side, but noticeably faded.

Machine Stitching

Use two basic machine stitches when you make your closet monsters: straight stitch and a zigzag stitch. Yes, I know you have a fancy, computerized machine, but this is what I suggest.

Find the stitch-length controls on your sewing machine. You may need to dust off the instruction manual and actually read it to know what's what. Look for a dial or lever with a series of numbers on or around it. It should be on the front of your machine toward the bottom right.

The number setting of the stitch-length control won't necessarily indicate how many stitches per inch are made at that setting. To determine the stitch lengths of your machine's

With this feeble coat hanger, I begin my conquest…

settings, find a long piece of scrap material like cotton shirting or light denim. Mark horizontal lines every inch of the scrap's length. Then test various stitch length settings by counting how many stitches your machine makes per inch at a particular setting. The default setting on my machine makes 11 stitches per inch through a piece of paper, and 12 stitches per inch through wool suiting.

Begin and end a line of stitching by hitting your machine's reverse button to lock your stitches in place. Knotting your threads is a pain, why bother?

Use the ranges given below as recommendations for length of your straight stitches. When in doubt, try stitching some scrap fabric to determine the best straight stitch length for your fabric. If your stitches are too long, they will not hold; if your stitches are too short, they will distort the fabric. Here are some simple tips for you to consider:

- Use the longest stitch-length setting to baste fabric pieces together, unless you're basting by hand with a running stitch.
- Choose a straight stitch on a sewing machine for woven fabrics such as denim, cotton shirting, corduroy, tweeds, suiting, and linings. Use a setting between 10 and 15 stitches per inch (which might very well be your machine's default setting). This produces a firm, secure seam.
- Sew medium-weight fabrics and knits such as lighter denims, velvet, corduroy, stretchy synthetics and sweatshirt knits with a stitch length of 10 to 12 stitches per inch.
- Use a stitch length of eight to 12 stitches per inch for heavy fabrics such as denim, vinyl, heavy wool, and suede.

Zigzag stitches and various overcast stitch settings are useful for helping prevent the raw edges of fabric from raveling. I primarily use zigzag stitches for sewing appliqués to a piece of fabric.

Zigzag stitches allow for some ease or stretch to stretchy fabrics. As we won't be wearing our stuffed toys, I'm less concerned about ease and stretch in our seams. But experiment with stitch length and width to create a stitch that works well with your fabric.

Seam Allowances

Seam allowance is the distance between the raw edge of your fabric and the line of stitching which binds your fabrics. I like to think of seam allowance as a halo surrounding the shape of an unsewn monster.

Seam allowance is necessary for secure, stable seams. If a seam is made too close to the raw edge of the fabrics, any normal wear to that fabric may cause raveling and fraying that could creep past the seam and make a hole. Seams should be $1/8$ to $5/8$ inch (3 mm to 1.5 cm) away from the fabric's raw edge to avoid any compromise due to raveling.

In general, use a $3/8$-inch (.95mm) seam allowance for the projects in this book unless otherwise specified. That said, you may want to allow for more seam allowance if your fabric ravels easily or use a smaller seam allowance if your fabric is light and tightly woven.

Yeah, so, use a sewing machine. Cause it's easier.

Hand Sewing

Basting or Running stitch: It's a stitch many tailors use to temporarily attach two pieces of fabric together, or to make ruffles and gathers.

Whip stitch: This stitch is the easiest overcast stitch you can do by hand. Many hand sewers use it as a quick and easy way to make a seam and to bind frayed edges.

Backstitch: This is one of my favorite hand stitches. When done properly and evenly, this stitch makes very sturdy, stable attachments, and even allows for its own ease when stuffing.

Anchoring Knot: This is the knot I use for anchoring my thread into place before starting a hand-sewn seam. It's sort of a nod to the French knot, which is primarily an embellishment. I also use this knot to tie off when I'm finished with a seam. You can, of course, anchor your thread however you like as long as your made-up knot looks nice and holds securely.

Closing Stitch: I've tried the ladder stitch and many variations and I admit that after all of my experience I'm still clunky at it. I've recently settled upon this stitch, which is my version of the baseball stitch. I like it because it looks nice. Since we have to close up a stuffing hole, and those closures are almost invariably visible, it's important to use a stitch that looks good.

Notching and Trimming

Once you've stitched your creature, and before you turn it right side out to stuff it, make sure your curves and corners are notched and trimmed.

Notching simply means you're going to use the tips of your fabric scissors to snip through the seam allowance, but not the seam itself. Cutting notches into the seam allowance along curves or at a corner will make the shape look smoother when it's turned right side out. Notch your curves about every quarter inch (6 mm) or so. Corners—like the valleys between fingers or crotches—need to be notched (at right).

Trimming reduces the width of seam allowances. As a general rule, trim all but 1/16-inch (1.5 mm) of seam allowance away from your corners. Narrow or pointed tubes like ears or tails need their seam allowances trimmed especially. Taper seam allowances on either side of a corner. It will make it easier to form a sharp corner when you turn it right side out (see figure at right).

If you don't trim these items, the seam allowance will start taking up space as you turn the item right side out. Towards the tip, the seam allowance will cause such bunching that turning the item right side out will eventually become impossible. Trim first for your sanity's sake

As you practice these techniques, make sure you don't cut into your seam by accident!

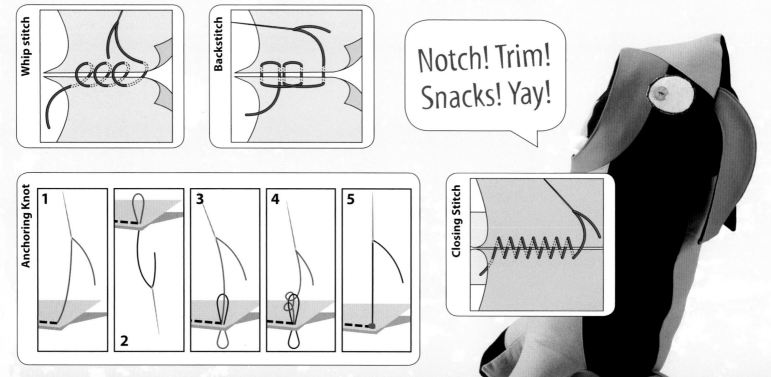

Whip stitch

Backstitch

Anchoring Knot
1
2
3
4
5

Closing Stitch

Notch! Trim! Snacks! Yay!

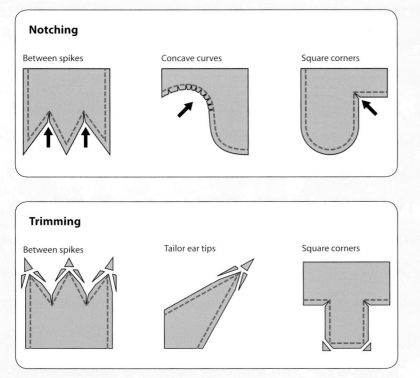

Notching

Between spikes   Concave curves   Square corners

Trimming

Between spikes   Tailor ear tips   Square corners

Stuffing

Stuffing a monster brings a mass of limp, stitched fabric to life. Adding beanbag filling to your creature gives a kind of lifelike weight and bounce to the end of an appendage. For the projects in this book, I recommend using just a few tablespoons of beanbag fill in an arm, foot, tail, or horn to give it the right amount of flop, weight, and bounce.

To get **beanbag fill** inside your creature without having it all over the floor, insert the spout of a kitchen funnel into the opening of your creature's arm, leg, or tail (see figure at right). If the appendage is already attached to your creature, maneuver the funnel into the stuffing hole, and scrunch your unstuffed creature till you can find the opening of the appendage and proceed from there. One or two tablespoons of beanbag fill are all you need for most appendages.

Stuff **polyester fiberfill** gradually. Add small pieces bit by bit. Avoid the temptation to cram large fistfuls of stuffing into your monster. First off, you'll never delicately fill a narrow limb or a tapering tail or tentacle all the way to the tip if you

cram. Cramming also causes nonuniform lumps and hard nodules, which look disquieting and tacky. Squish and massage fiberfill as you go to ensure even distribution of the stuffing. Fill your creature thoroughly and as firmly as you like. Respect the limits of your fabric. If you're using fabric that doesn't stretch, don't put pressure on its seams by overfilling it. Creatures made from stretchy fabric can take more stuffing.

Using **scrap fabric** for fill is best used inside creature heads and bodies as a supplement to fiberfill. Scraps do take space up, but aren't great for filling out details. If I were using scrap fabric as fill, I'd go ahead and fill my creature with fiberfill, then add the scraps to give the creature more volume.

If you're stuffing an entire body at once—one that, perhaps, has horns or long ears at the top—start with small bits of stuffing and stuff the long extremities first, working your way into the head and down the neck. Stop and stuff any arms the creature might have. Wherever your fingers can't reach, use the closed tip of your scissors, a pencil, or a 1/4-inch (6 mm) wooden dowel. Continue stuffing the creature down through the torso, then finish with the legs

Once your creature is closed up, you can further squash and gently distribute the stuffing around inside it. Give your creature a rest for a day—he's been through an ordeal! The stuffing and fibers will relax and the creature's shape will settle.

Filling

Closet Monster Anatomy

Arms

I'm using two basic arm construction methods in this book. Once you've learned them, you can apply your own genius and vary them till you go stark raving mad and your friends hold an intervention for you. I will give suggested measurements for the sizes of the components needed for these kinds of arms. Ultimately, the more you design, the more you'll see what works for you.

The Gusseted Palm

I know, this sounds like a resort for full-figured vacationers, but it, in fact, isn't. It's a simple tube shape with an added gusset.

1. Cut a rectangle and a triangle. Make their top edges match. Keep the triangle significantly shorter than the rectangle, by perhaps half (see figure A1).

2. With right sides facing, align one side of the triangle to the corresponding side of the rectangle and stitch into place. Leave a ³⁄₈-inch (.95 cm) seam allowance (see figure A2).

3. Fold your newly attached pieces over and match the edges to the rectangle's opposite edge (see figure A3). Pin the edges into position and stitch them together leaving ³⁄₈-inch (.95 cm) seam allowance (see figure A4).

4. You should have a tapering form that looks something like the letter Y when wrong side out (see figure A5).

5. Flatten your arm and arrange the triangle so that it's directly in the middle, and facing you. Match its top edge with the top edge of the rectangle. Use a fabric pen or tailor's chalk to draw a wide "W" spanning its entire width, but about ¼-inch (6 mm) below the top edges (see figure A6).

6. Stitch right on your "W" line. Go through all the layers of your arm, and make sure you start and end your stitching right at the edges (see figure A7).

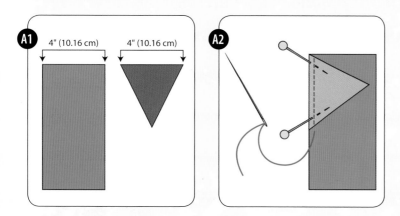

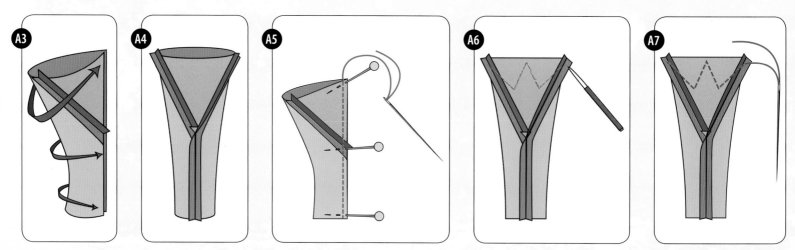

7. Trim the excess material around the "W". Remember to notch the inside corners of your "W" (see figure A8). Turn your arm right side out (see figure A9). Stuff your arm thoroughly but not over-firm. Leave ½ inch (1.3 cm) of space unstuffed at the opening of your arm.

8. Attach this arm to your creature at the side seam of its torso using the Tuck and Sew method found on page 30. If you're using thick or stretchy material, you can attach this arm to your creature using the Circumference method found on page 31.

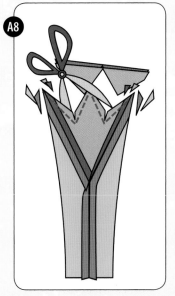

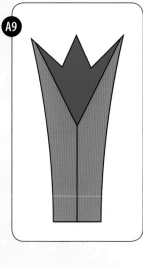

The Freefinger

This arm method is pretty simple. It's a great one for illustrating what seam allowance is, how it functions and how it affects your finished piece.

1.   Start with two rectangles approximately 4 inches (10 cm) wide and 10 inches (25 cm) long and align them together with right sides facing (see figure A10).

2.   Use a fabric pen to draw whatever kind of fingery arm you want on one of the rectangles. Make sure that your fingers are no narrower than 1-inch (2.5 cm) wide and at least ¼ inch

(6 mm) apart to allow for adequate seam allowance (see figure A11). Pin the rectangles together and stitch along the line you drew (see figure A12).

3.   Trim the excess fabric off of the arm, leaving a suitable seam allowance for the fabric you're using. Make sure you notch the corners and curves between the fingers (see figure A13). Turn the arm right side out (see figure A14).

4.   Insert beanbag filling into the fingers before stuffing with fiberfill. Leave ½ inch (1.3 cm) of space unstuffed at the arm's opening. Attach this arm on a side seam of its torso using the Tuck and Sew method found on page 30. If you're using thick or stretchy material, attach the arm using the Circumference method found on page 31.

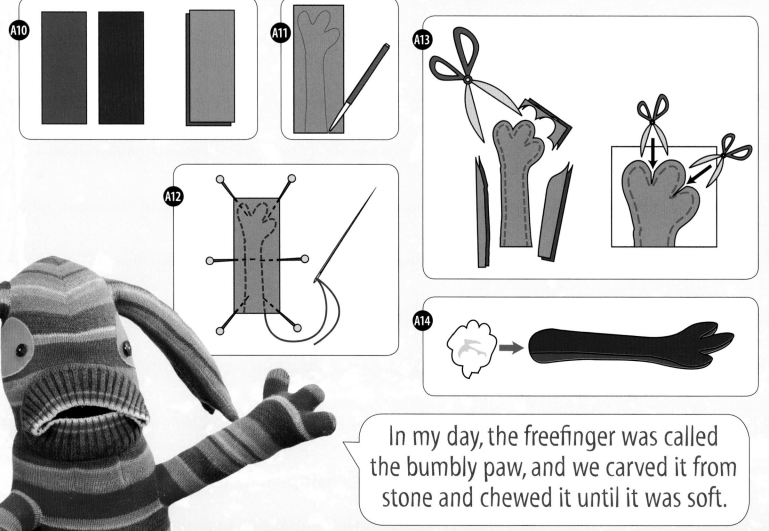

In my day, the freefinger was called the bumbly paw, and we carved it from stone and chewed it until it was soft.

Legs

Here are a few methods I've found to make legs. Once you're used to these basic steps, you can vary them as much as you like. Please, feel free to give your monster as many legs you want. Who couldn't use another pair?

The Basic Dangly Leg

This leg is a simple boot shape. You'll sew it into the bottom seam of your creature's body and let it flop around. A few scoops of beanbag fill in the toe will add a nice, weighty bounce to the leg.

1. Start with a wide rectangle approximately 5 x 8 inches (12.7 x 20.3 cm). Fold it in half, matching the shorter edges (see figure L1).

2. Draw the profile of an ankle and foot using the fold in the fabric as the back of your leg. Stitch along the line you drew (see figure L2).

3. Cut the excess fabric away from your foot leaving enough seam allowance to suit the fabric you're using. Keep these pieces. They might make good ears (see figure L3).

4. To make a sole for this foot, follow the instructions for stitching a bottom found on page 28.

5. Turn your foot right side out and stuff it. If you want to add beanbag fill, do that first. Refer to the beanbag instructions found on page 17. Leave ½ inch (1.3 cm) of space unstuffed at the opening (see figure L4). Attach this leg to your creature at the bottom seam of its torso using the Tuck and Sew method found on page 30.

L1

Wide rectangle

Fold it in half.

L3

L2

Folded edge

Folded edge

L4

On my planet, we just floated.
But I do like walking.

The Dangly Leg with a Different Colored Toe and No Sole

This is a great looking leg that's easy to make. Like the basic dangly leg, this one's going to be sewn into the seam at the bottom of your creature so it can flop around. Use some beanbag fill in this leg, too, for some weight and bounce.

1. You will need a long strip of fabric approximately 10 inches (25.4 cm) long and 3 inches (7.6 cm) thick, and a half-oval or a triangle about 4 inches (10 cm) at its base and perhaps 4 inches (10 cm) tall (see figure L5).

With right sides touching, align the flat base of the toe piece to the exact middle of one of the wide edges of the leg strip and stitch the two pieces together. Leave a seam allowance that suits the fabric you're using (see figure L6).

2. Fold the leg in half, matching the short ends of the leg strip with right sides touching (see figure L7).

3. Pin the edges of the leg and foot, securing the edges and corners. Pin together the seams where the base of the toe meets the leg (see figure L8).

4. Stitch from the short ends of the leg strip down the back of the leg, and down the front of the leg, and over the toe. Remember to notch the corner where the toe meets the leg (see figure L9).

5. Turn the leg right side out and stuff it. Leave ½ inch (1.3 cm) of unstuffed space at the opening of the leg. If you want beanbag filling in the toe, put that in first. Find instructions for inserting beanbag fill on page 17 (see figure L10). Attach this leg to your creature at the bottom seam of its torso using the Tuck and Sew method found on page 30.

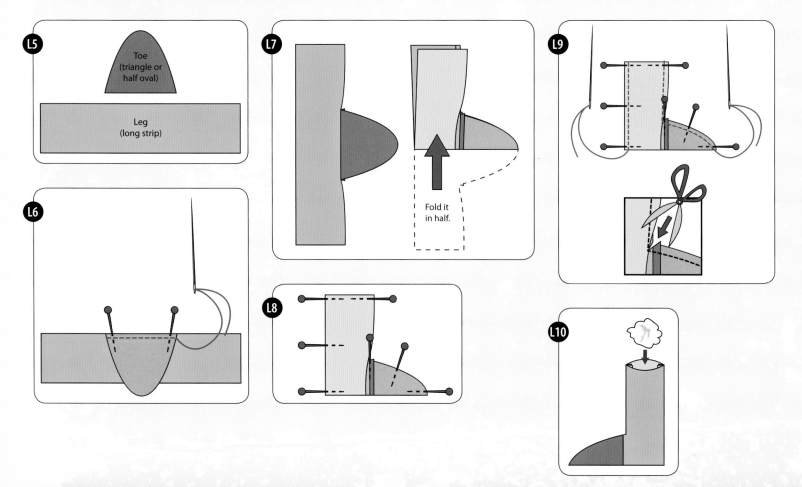

L5 — Toe (triangle or half oval) / Leg (long strip)
L6
L7 — Fold it in half.
L8
L9
L10

The Stub

This leg is perhaps the easiest leg to make and it isn't the result of a lawn care incident! These legs are a continuation of your creature's body. So make 'em as short (or long) as you want. You can even give these legs soles if you want (see page 28).

1. Look at the piece of fabric you've cut for your creature's torso. Decide how much is to become the body and how much will become the length of legs you envision.

2. Cut a crotch by snipping a line perpendicular to the base of your creature's body. Make the line as long as you want your legs to be (see figure L11). You can give the legs a wider stance by cutting a rectangle out of your creature's torso instead of just cutting a line. If you choose this route, please be sure that the legs you have left are wide enough to turn and stuff. Let 3 inches (7.6 cm), plus seam allowance, be a rule of thumb for leg width (see figure L11).

3. Take this opportunity to appliqué toenails onto the bottoms of the feet if you want them. See the appliqué instructions on page 33 (see figure L12).

4. Sew from the edge of one foot up across the crotch, and down to the edge of the other foot. Leaving enough seam allowance to suit the fabric you're using (see figure L13).

5. You can close off the bottoms of the legs by simply sewing them straight across, sewing a rounded curve, or sewing a zigzaggy, claw-like seam (see figure L14).

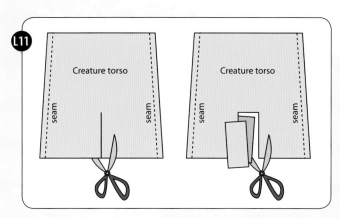

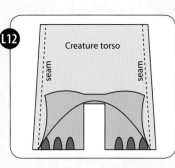

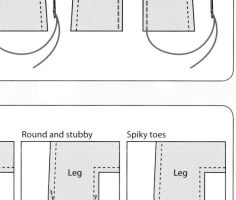

The Add-A-Stub

This leg method is an effective way to add a stocky leg nub to a creature's long torso.

1. Fold leg rectangles in half with wrong sides touching (see figure L15).

2. With the torso wrong side out, slide the folded leg rectangles into the torso. The right sides of the legs and torso should touch. Match the pinned midpoints of the leg rectangles with the side seams of the creature's torso (see figure L16).

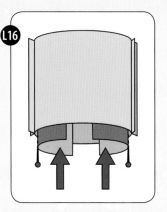

3. Stitch the edges of the legs and torso together leaving a suitable seam allowance for the fabric you're using (see figure L17).

4. Remove the pins and pull the legs out of the torso. Place new pins in the corners and edges of the legs, and in the seam where the leg meets the torso. Stitch the open edge of both legs, and leave the crotch open for stuffing (see figure L18).

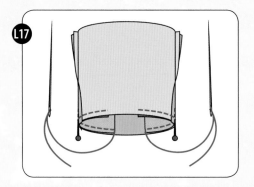

5. You can close off the bottoms of the legs by simply sewing them straight across, sewing a rounded curve, or sewing a zigzaggy, claw-like seam (see figure L14 on page 23). Feel free to create your own toe design if you prefer.

6. To cap these feet with a round bottom, refer to the creature bottoms instructions on page 28.

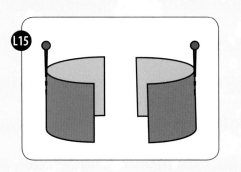

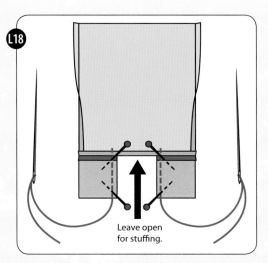

Leave open
for stuffing.

Ears, Horns, and Head Thingies

Something I like a lot about making closet monsters is that even the scraps from your projects have great potential and value. Narrow strips make great long, striped head tentacles; folded cuffs or pocket closures are handy ready-made thingies. Here are a few head protuberances that will make your creature sit up and listen.

The Serendipitous Ear

Are you listening? Any and everything you have leftover from disassembly can be used for extra body parts and features. This ear is just one of the bajillions of different uses for fabric scraps.

1. Find two fabric remnants of similar size. They don't have to be similar in substance. Different colors are ideal. Align them as best you can with right sides touching (see figure E1).

2. Trim the remnants to the same size and shape. Keep one edge of the shape a straight line (see figure E2).

3. Pin the remnants to a piece of batting, fleece, or sweatshirt material for padding. Sew through all layers of the fabric and padding, leaving a seam allowance that suits the most sensitive material you're using (see figure E3).

4. Remove your pins and trim the padding to the same size and shape of your ear. Trim any tight corners and notch any concave curves at this point (see figure E4).

5. Turn the ear right side out making sure that the padding winds up between the two layers of fabric. Do this carefully in case your ear material is prone to fray (see figure E5).

6. Stitch a border around the ear about ⅜-inch (.95cm) from the edge (see figure E6). Now you're done!

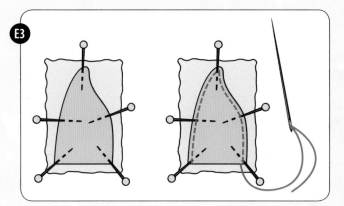

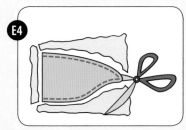

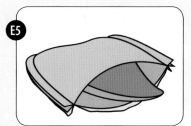

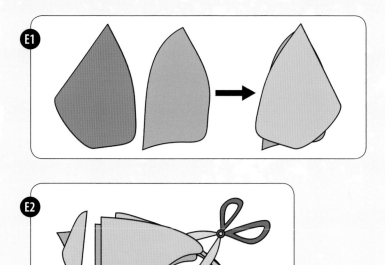

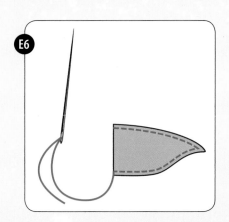

The Mentacle

You can call this mental tentacle an ear, a horn, or a whatsit for all I care. As you'll see throughout the projects in this book, this is one of my favorite head treatments.

1. From two different colored (but otherwise similar) fabrics, cut eight to 10 strips of fabric roughly 6 inches (10 cm) long by 2½ inches (6.3 cm) wide (see figure M1).

2. Combine half the strips of one color with half the strips of the other, and arrange them alternately (see figure M2).

3. Sew the long edges of the fabric together, with right sides touching, until you've sewn all the stripes together (see figure M3).

4. If you want, trim the rectangular ears into a taper so that your ears will come to a point when sewn shut (see figure M4). Attach the mentacle to your creature's head, following the instructions for the Arc method found on page 30.

The As-Is

Even more serendipitous than the Serendipitous Ear, this ear-making technique uses ready-made parts of old clothing. Detach a pocket flap or a shirt cuff from a piece of clothing. Fold it in half or however you want; see the ears on Lurwin or BooFaye (pages 44 and 126 respectively). Attach it to your creature's head using the Tuck and Sew method found on page 30.

A Horn of Your Own

1. For the basic horn, find remnants of identical fabric and align them with right sides facing (see figure H1).

2. Cut out a horn-like shape. Make sure you account for seam allowance and cut the shape sufficiently wide for turning and stuffing after stitching (see figure H2).

3. Stitch the shapes together leaving adequate seam allowance. Don't forget to notch any curves and trim the point (see figure H3).

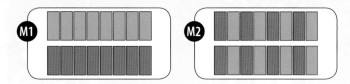

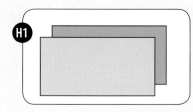

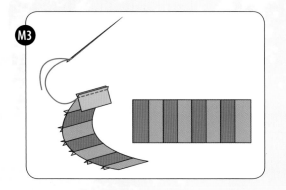

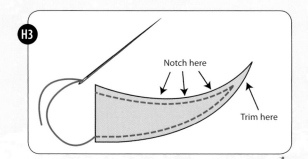

Notch here

Trim here

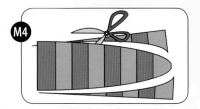

Buck Teeth

1. Cut a wide rectangle, approximately 6 x 2 inches (15 x 5 cm) out of your favorite tooth-colored fabric. Anything light and pale works well for this.

2. Fold the rectangle in half with right sides facing, aligning the wide edges together (see figure T1).

3. From the open edges, stitch as many U shapes as you can, in a row. You can fit probably no more than four teeth on a fabric swatch this size. Leave ¼ inch (6 mm) seam allowance in between each tooth, and no less than ⅛-inch (3 mm) seam allowance between their bottom curves and folded edges (see figure T2).

4. Cut the teeth apart by slicing the seam allowance between them. Trim the corners of the seam allowance at their bottom curves (see figure T3).

5. Turn the teeth right side out (it will look like a teeny tiny bag) and stuff them lightly (see figure T4).

6. Attach the teeth to your monster's face using the Tuck and Sew method found on page 30. Specific monster projects will show you exactly where to attach teeth like this.

Lickers

1. Cut a 2 x 4½-inch (5 x 12 cm) rectangle of your favorite tongue-looking fabric. Fold the strip short end to short end, with right sides touching (see figures T5 and T6).

2. Stitch the raw edges together in a rounded or tapering U-formation. The curve of the U should be at the fold of the strip. Trim the corners off the curve of your tongue, and turn it right side out (see figure T7). Lightly stuff the tongue.

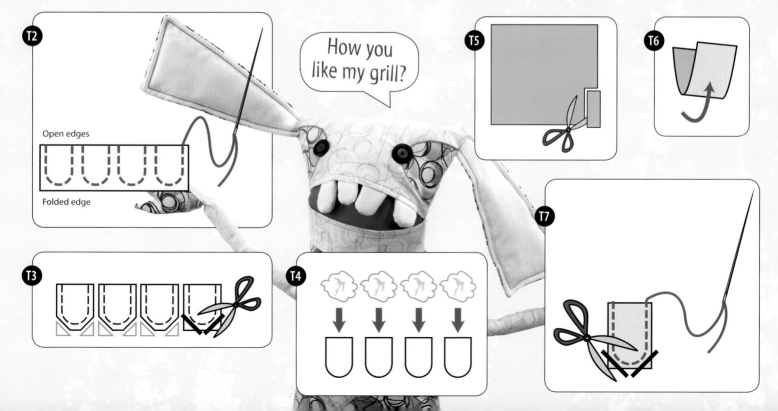

T1

T2
Open edges
Folded edge

How you like my grill?

T5

T6

T3

T4

T7

Make it plump, but not huge. Don't pack it or round it out. You want it to stay basically flat (see figure T8).

3. Take the stuffed tongue and stitch a straight line from the open end to within 3/16 inch (5 mm) from the tip (see figure T9). This makes a reasonably convincing tongue-ish crease. Use the Tuck and Sew method on page 30 to attach your tongue.

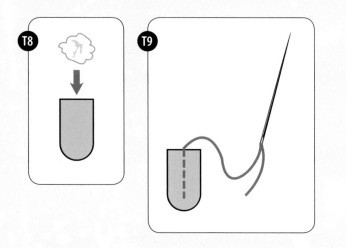

Eyes
Recycler that I am, I repurpose buttons and scraps for eyes. To make them stand out, I add a bit of appliqué.

1. Cut a nice piece of accent fabric, often from lining or pocket interiors, into a big or little, round or whatever eye shape to give your creature a pop of cartoon expression. Appliqué the shaped onto the creature before you sew the creature together using a zigzag stitch or, if you forget, stitch it on by hand after you assemble and stuff it.

2. Use the buttons as pupils for an effective focal point. I like to layer buttons of different sizes and colors to give a creature a bewildered gaze.

All this appliqué does nothing for my depth perception.

Presenting Creature Feature Bottoms!
Some of the creatures in this book have big round bottoms or soles on their feet. I'll show you how to make butts for your creatures that will help them sit up all by themselves. Once you've mastered monster butts, the very same methods can be applied to the soles of feet. You'll need to have finished your creature's body or torso. You'll also need a square of fabric to match the torso width and a calculator. Caution: pi is involved, but not the kind you eat!

1. Lay the bottom opening of your creature's body flat on a work surface. Measure the width of the entire bottom edge, including both seam allowances (see figure B1). If the width of the bottom edge is 12 inches (30.5 cm), it's best to cut a 13-inch (33 cm) square of fabric for your bottom. A sleeve or part of a pants leg will work for this. They're usually big enough.

2. Now, divide that width by 3.14 (pi) to determine the radius of the circle you'll need to make. If the number, for example, is 3.82, that's roughly 3⅞ inches (9.8 cm), so you may as well make your measurement 4 inches (10.2 cm) just to be on the safe side. You can always trim your bottom down, but there's no magic that will make it bigger, unless you want to start over.

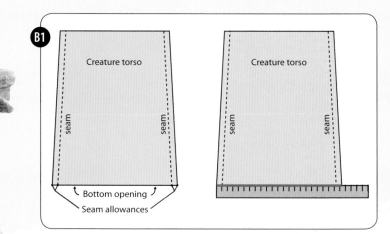

3. Fold your square of fabric into even quarters. Press the folds with an iron for best results. Use a ruler to measure the radius you calculated out from the folded corner. Mark that measurement with a fabric pen. Now, rotate the ruler and mark more points until you reach the adjacent edge of your folded fabric (see figure B2). Connect the dots!

4. Slip a pin or two in the folded fabric to keep the layers from shifting, and cut the fabric along the connected dots. Unpin and unfold the fabric, and you'll have a circle.

5. Place pins at its edges at noon, 3, 6, and 9 o'clock to help you align it properly with the bottom edge of your monster's body (see figure B3).

NOTE: Before you attach your creature's bottom to its body, take a peek at the specific instructions so you know when to attach any legs or appendages. Inserting appendages comes before attaching bottoms, and each project will tell you when to do that.

6. Keep your creature's body wrong side out. Align the bottom so that its right side faces down into the body, like snapping on a jar lid. Use the pins in the edges of your creature's bottom to help you align it properly to the torso (see figure B4). If you're making foot soles, this step might not be necessary.

7. Place as many pins as you feel are necessary to hold the bottom properly in place once it's aligned. I'm personally a pin-o-holic, so when I attach my creature bottoms it's a full-on disco ball pin party. Sew around the edges of the torso and bottom. Refer to the instructions of the project you're making to know if you need to leave a stuffing hole here or not. If you do need to leave a stuffing hole, leave a good 4 inches (10.2 cm) of space unsewn at this attachment, preferably at the back or side (see figure B5).

Oval Bottoms

Some of the creatures in this book have oval bottoms. Maureen McDoover (page 88) is a very good example.

1. Make a circle with a diameter (not radius) as wide as the entire bottom edge of your creature's body, including both seam allowances (see figure B1 on the previous page).

2. Decide how thick you want your oval to be. Do you want a skinny monster or a chunkier monster? Fold your circle in half. Trim the half circle so the edge has a flatter curve (see figure B6). Don't make any cuts on the fold line! Err on making the oval larger than you want—it's easier to snip away some fabric to fit than having to cut another circle.

3. Follow the steps for round bottoms to attach the oval to your creature.

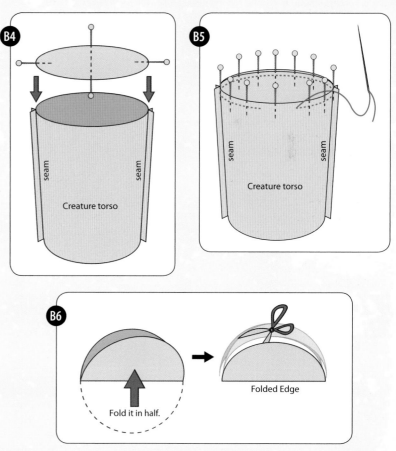

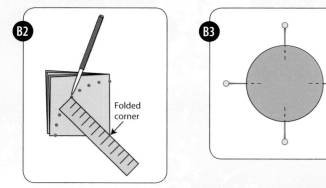

Attaching Limbs and Other Body Parts

The Tuck and Sew Method

This attachment method can be used with any fabric. It holds your creature's limbs, ears, tongues, teeth, or whatever firmly in place while allowing them to flop around freely.

1. Insert a finished and stuffed body part such as an ear or an arm in between two layers of fabric. Match the raw edges of the appendage with the raw edges of the fabric (see figure P1).

2. Stitch the layers of fabric together at the edge with the item in between, securing the item to the seam (see figure P1).

The Arc Method

This miraculous attachment method lets you add an appendage to a seam without stitching shut the opening of the appendage (as with the Tuck and Sew method explained previously). Rather than flopping or dangling, the body part will have a rounded base and appear to grow out of the creature's head or body. Just the way nature intended it to.

1. Start with a partially sewn creature head or torso. Arrange the front and back panels of the torso together with right sides facing. Stitch down both sides of the torso from the top edge until you reach the point where you think the appendage ought to go, and stop. We'll call the end of those seams Point A (see figure P2).

2. Fold the appendage you wish to attach in half vertically, with wrong sides touching. Place a pin at the fold of the edge that will attach to the creature. We'll call this pin Point B (see figure P3).

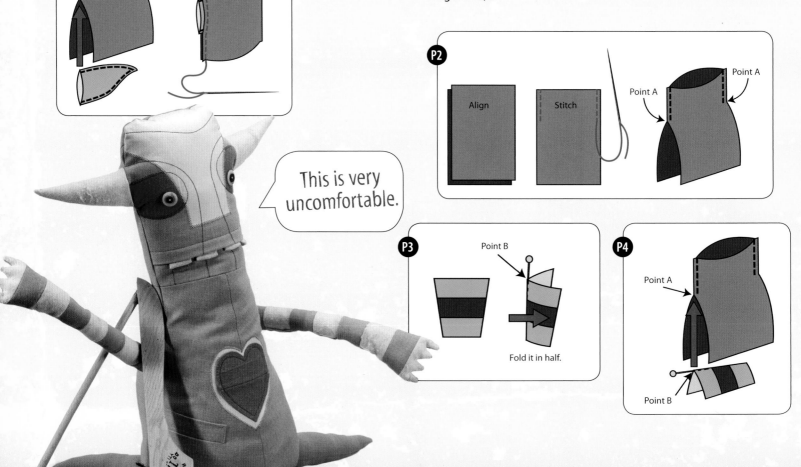

This is very uncomfortable.

3. Insert the appendage between the two layers of the creature's head or torso, with right sides touching. Align Point B on the appendage with point A on the head or body (see figure P4).

4. Hand stitch the edge of the appendage to the edge of the head or body, stopping at Point A. Flip the creature to its back side and repeat (see figure P5). Do this again to attach an appendage to the other side of the head or body.

5. Pull the appendages out from inside the creature, making everything wrong side out. Align edges and seams together and secure with pins. Stitch down the long edge of the appendage to the point where it attaches to the creature. Turn and stitch down the torso, finishing its side seam (see figure P6).

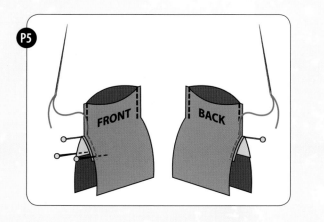

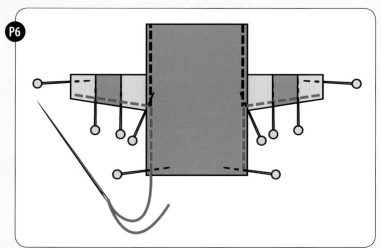

The Circumference Method

This attachment method is best used with stretchy, knit fabrics. It lets you add an appendage directly onto fabric by cutting a hole. I use this method for limbs such as arms and horns. If your fabric has no stretch to it, use a different attachment method, as this one requires the forgiving qualities of stretchiness.

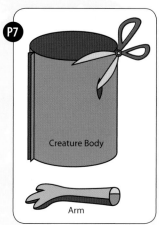

1. With your creature's body wrong side out, cut a tiny slit where you want the arm to attach. Widen the slit as necessary to accommodate the opening of the limb you want to attach. Do this by snipping a few fibers of the fabric, and gently prying the hole wider with your scissors. It's best to start out with a hole that's too small for your limb. Widen it a bit at a time until the hole is the right size (see figure P7).

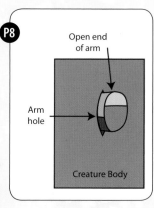

2. Keep the limb right side out. Stick it up inside the body, and match its opening to the slit you cut. Use pins as necessary (see figure P8).

3. Here's where the stretchiness of the fabric comes in handy. You'll need to cajole the edges of the hole you cut to match the edges of the limb's opening. Once you've matched both edges, stitch securely and carefully around them leaving ³⁄₈-inch (.95 cm) seam allowance. A few rounds of hand stitching with whip stitches make a very sturdy attachment, but this can be done by machine if you're careful (see figure P9).

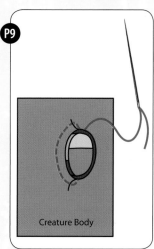

4. Stuff the limb when you stuff the rest of the creature.

The Bubble Method

The bubble method may be a little tricky, but if you can visualize the way two soap bubbles look when they're stuck together, it's a cinch. You'll use this method almost exclusively for heads, but that doesn't mean you can't use it for ears, arms, and what-have-you. I'll walk you through attaching a head.

1. You'll need the front and back of your creature's head, and the front and back of the creature's body. Be sure that any appliqué for facial features has been done before you assemble your creature with this method (see figure P10).

2. Place the back of the head atop the front of the body, with right sides touching (see figure P11).

Draw an oval where the two shapes overlap. The oval will need to be the right size to allow for seam allowance outside the oval and inside the edges of the shapes (see figure P11).

3. Pin the shapes together as necessary and stitch them together around the oval you drew (see figure P12).

4. Snip out the oval you drew. Cut through both the head and the body (see figure P13).

5. Pull the body through the hole so that its wrong side now touches the wrong side of the head. This step is probably the trickiest part of the bubble method, but if you just trust the instructions and try it, you'll understand it completely (see figure P14).

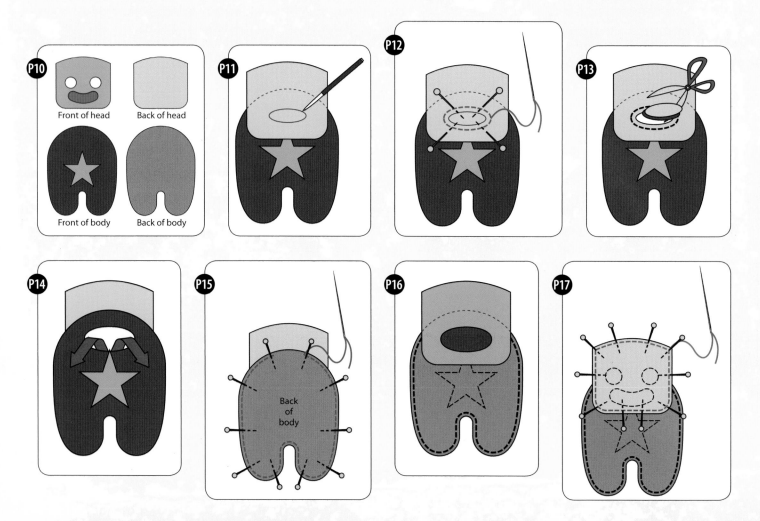

P10 — Front of head / Back of head / Front of body / Back of body
P11
P12
P13
P14
P15 — Back of body
P16
P17

6. Lay the back of the body atop the front of the body with right sides touching. Stitch the two together around the edges, leaving enough seam allowance to suit the fabric you're using (see figure P15).

Leave a 4-inch (10 cm) unstitched space somewhere on the body for turning and stuffing (see figure P15).

7. Turn the project over so that the right side of the head now faces forward (see figure P16).

8. Place the front of the head (the face) atop the back of the head with right sides touching. Stitch all the way around the edges (see figure P17).

Oh-So-Special Touches

Add decorative details to your creature's exterior with appliqué or artistic top-stitching. Both are best done early as you prepare the parts of your creature.

Appliqué

Appliqué is a great design solution for facial features, fingernails, hearts, stars, and more! There are lots of ways to appliqué—by hand or machine. I'm fond of using fusible adhesive webbing to keep my shapes in place as I sew them.

1. Trim the adhesive webbing to the same size as your accent fabric (see figure Q1).

2. Follow the manufacturer's instructions for ironing (or fusing) the webbing to the wrong side of your fabric.

3. Cut the accent fabric to the shape you want (see figure Q2). Peel away the backing paper.

4. Place the cut appliqué onto your fabric and iron it into place.

5. Once your appliqué is ironed into place, use an overcast stitch or whip stitch to permanently attach it to the monster fabric. (see figure Q3).

Top-Stitching

I like adding decorative top-stitching to my monster's parts while they're still just flat shapes of fabric. I use it to add detail to faces or some interest to a torso or a bit of fabric that could use some flair.

Top-stitching can be used to add some tension to stretchy fabric and knits. When the creature is stuffed, the top-stitching remains taut and the fabric around it fills out, giving the monster creases and details. Stuff gently so you won't pop the stitches when stuffing your creature.

To top-stitch, use a straight stitch on your sewing machine, or a backstitch with your thread and needle. Keep your stitches small. Draw the shape or pattern you wish to stitch directly on the wrong side of the fabric if you wish. Me? I like drawing directly with the sewing machine.

Now that we've covered all the basics, let's get started on some creatures!

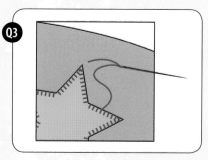

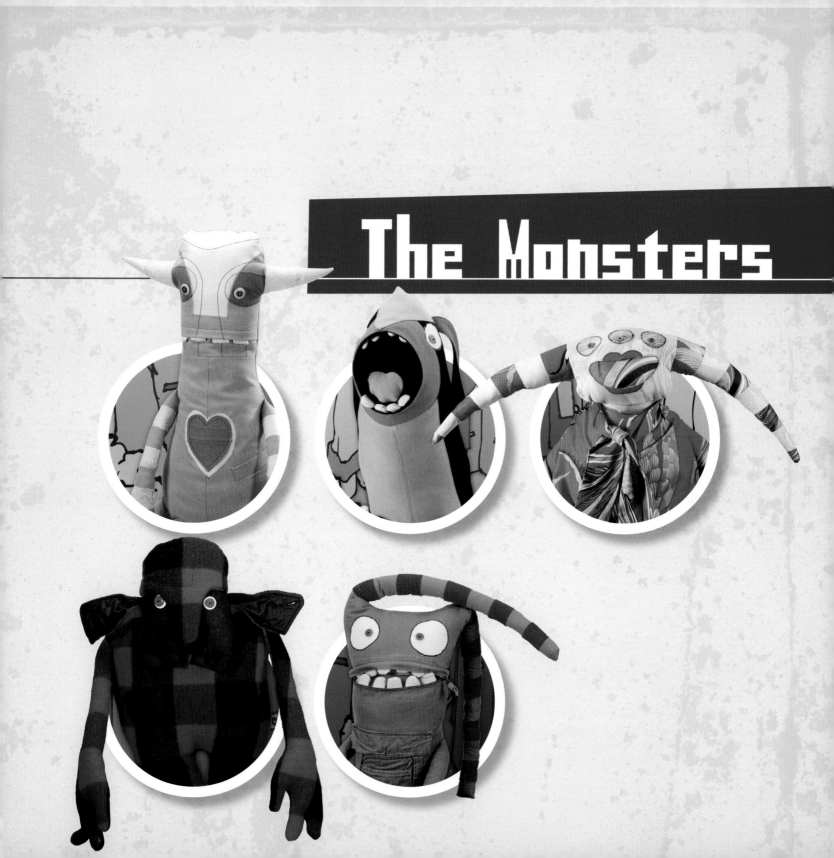

The Monsters

Flapp and Cuff

Flapp and Cuff are twin partners in pranks and both have a juvenile sense of humor: they sneak into restaurants and loosen the lids of salt and pepper shakers or switch the signs on public restrooms. Like most siblings, Flapp always gets away with murder while Cuff gets stuck with the cleanup and the blame.

{ *My brother and I were close enough in age to make sorting clothes a problem, so we grew up with all of our stuff color-coded. More often than not, his things were blue, my things were red. When I saw these button-down shirts, I wanted to make not one monster, but a pair of siblings.* }

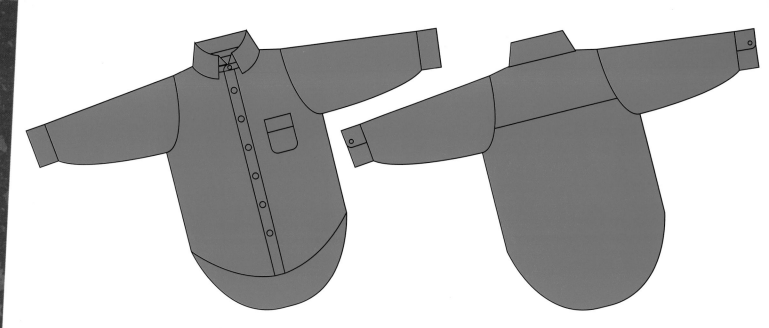

Prepare to make your twins by disassembling a couple of button-down shirts as shown in the Disassembly Chart. The two shirts should be similar in fiber content, stretch, and texture. Shirts of contrasting or clashing colors are ideal for making these twins.

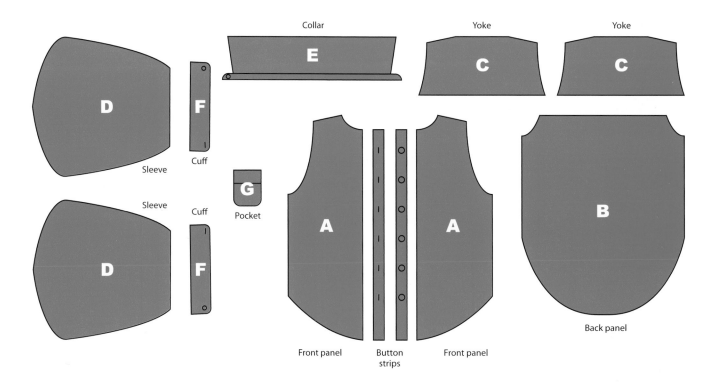

Collar

E

Yoke

C

Yoke

C

D

F

Sleeve

Cuff

G

Pocket

A

A

B

Sleeve

Cuff

D

F

Front panel

Button strips

Front panel

Back panel

1. Here we go. Align all four parts A from both shirts along the edge where the buttons used to be. Match the shoulder and arm curves as best you can. Cut horizontally where indicated to create a rectangle from the remaining midriff (see figures 1A and 1B).

2. Button both of the detached collars (parts E). Press them flat and measure the bottom edge as shown. Add ¾ inch (1.9 cm) to your measurement. Trim the width of the midriff parts to match this measurement (see figure 1C).

3. Cut the rectangle horizontally about one-third of the way down from the top. You'll use the larger rectangles for the bodies and the smaller ones for the heads of your creatures (see figure 1D).

4. Grab the four chest pieces you removed from the midriff in step 1. Trim the sleeve and shoulder edges as shown to create a rectangle. Cut the resulting rectangles in half to create eight rectangles. Reserve one pair of rectangles (per color) for arms; the other pairs will become the legs (see figures 1E and 1F).

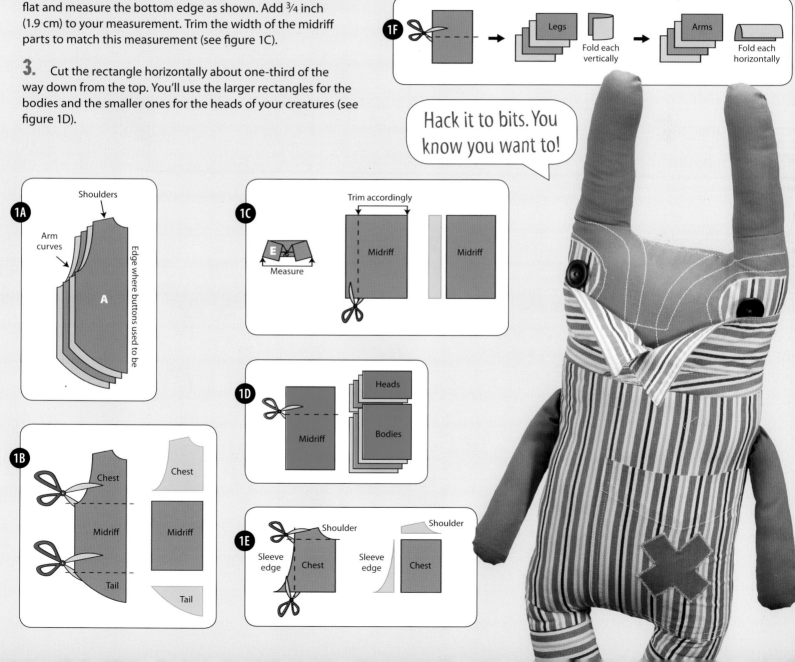

1F Legs / Fold each vertically → Arms / Fold each horizontally

Hack it to bits. You know you want to!

1A Shoulders / Arm curves / A / Edge where buttons used to be

1C Trim accordingly / E / Measure / Midriff / Midriff

1D Midriff / Heads / Bodies

1B Chest / Midriff / Tail / Chest / Midriff / Tail

1E Shoulder / Sleeve edge / Chest / Shoulder / Sleeve edge / Chest

5. To make the tall ears, start by trimming one sleeve from each shirt (part D) into even rectangles. Cut the rectangles into horizontal halves (see figures 1G, 1H, and 1I).

We've cut all the parts we need for the misbehaving twins. You should have heaps of parts leftover from the shirts you disassembled. Don't toss them out. Use them for other projects. I used scraps and remnants for appliqué on the twins' faces and pockets.

6. Look at figure 1J for an overview of the body parts we've cut and how they'll be arranged to make the twins. Arrange your parts and plan any appliqués you may want to add to your creature. I like to add simple rounded shapes on the head to define the eyes. Perhaps you'll want to add other facial features. Even more importantly, now is the time to stitch any appliqué before you start stitching the body together. Refer to page 33 for appliqué and top-stitching tips, and look at figure 1K for additional appliqué ideas.

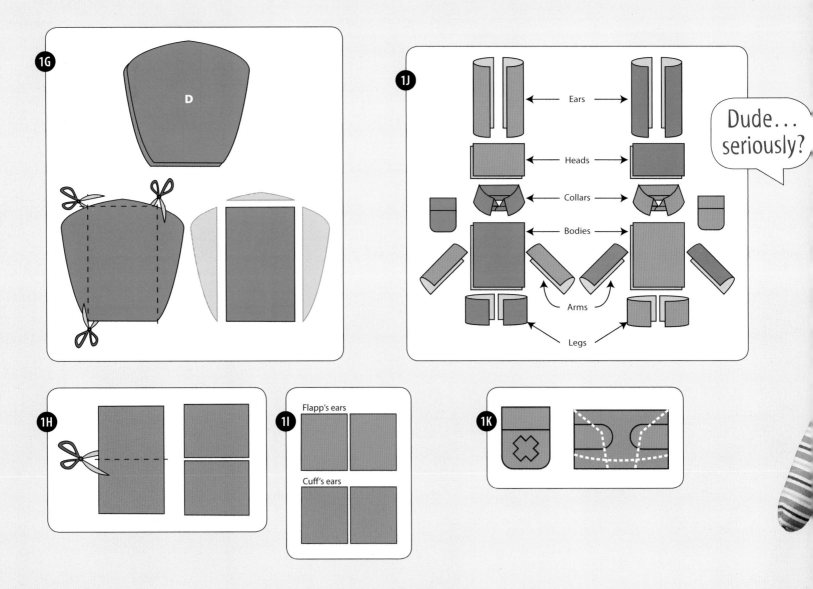

Stitching

7. First, let's make the arms. Fold the rectangles you cut for the arms matching long edge to long edge, with right sides touching. Stitch the raw edges together, leaving one end open. Stitch a curve into the closed end and trim the corners. Trim the seam allowance along the curved edge (see page 16 for trimming tips). You can stuff the arms completely with fiberfill, but I like to add some beanbag fill (see page 17) to the closed ends to give them some weighted flop and bounce (see figure 1L).

8. Grab one of the pockets you detached from the shirts, and reattach it to the part you cut for the front of your creature's body. Place it wherever you want it to go. Don't stitch around all of its edges if you want to preserve its function as a pocket! There should be evident stitch marks on the pocket's edges to show how it was sewn on before. Stitch along those marks and you'll be good to go (see figure 1M).

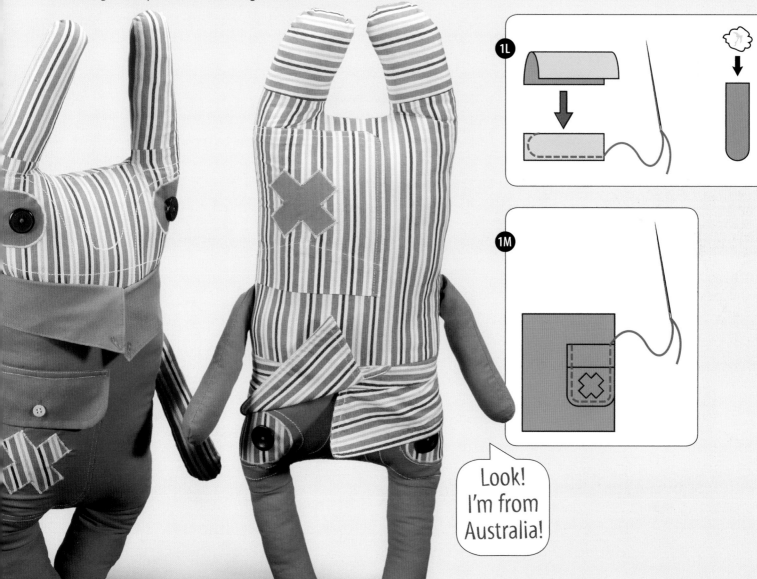

Look! I'm from Australia!

9. Lay the front of the body atop the back of the body with right sides facing. Insert the arms between the body layers wherever you think the arms ought to go. I angled my creatures' arms downward. You can angle yours upward or straight to the sides if you want to. Pin the corners of your body layers together, and pin the arms into place between them. Stitch the sides of the body together, clamping the arms into place. Trim any excess arm material if you have lots of overhang like I did (see figures 1N and 1O). Set the body aside for now.

10. Lay the face of your monster atop the back of its head with right sides touching. Stitch the side edges together with a $3/8$-inch (.95 cm) seam allowance (see figure 1P). Turn the head right side out and set it aside.

11. Remove the button from the collar of the shirt you took apart, then pin or baste the closure shut again. We want the collar closed, and we'll be stitching right where the button was. Pop the collar straight up (see figure 1Q). Turn the collar upside down, and stick it inside the body. Align the front of the collar with the center of the body's front, and match the edges. Now turn the head upside down, and insert it into the collar inside the body. Make sure the face of the creature touches the front of the collar, and the front of the creature's body. Pin the whole assembly in place along the top edges, aligning the side seams of the head and body together. Stitch all the edges together leaving a $3/8$-inch (.95 cm) seam allowance (see figures 1R and 1S). Whew!

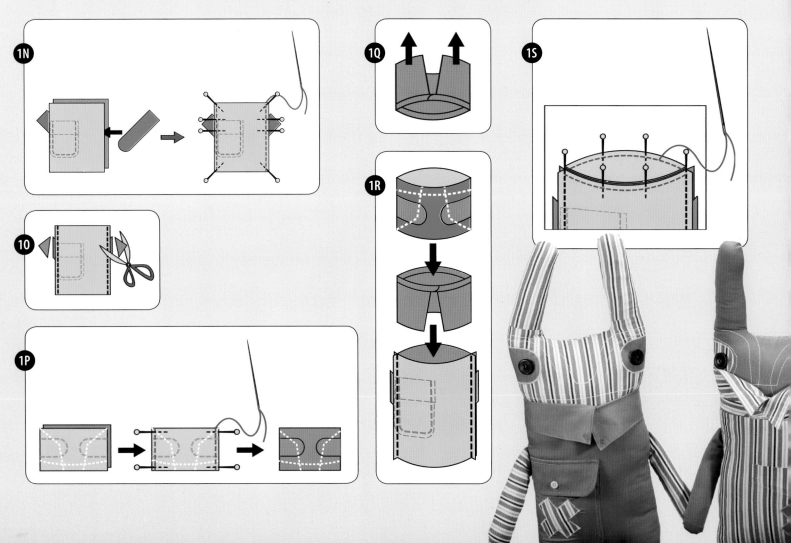

12. Pull the head out from inside the body and grab the rectangles you're using for ears. Even though it's called a leg method, follow the Add-A-Stub instructions on page 24 to attach the ears (see figure 1T).

13. Pull the ears out from inside the head. Pin and stitch them shut, following the Add-A-Stub leg attachment method from page 16. You're welcome to make the ears pointed or pronged like fingers if you wish. Remember to trim your points and notch any corners or curves (see page 16 for notching and trimming tips). Leave the space at the top of the head, between the ears, unstitched so you can stuff your creature later (see figure 1U).

14. Grab the rectangles you cut for your creatures' legs. Follow the Add-A-Stub leg instructions to stitch the legs to your creature, just like you did the ears. Feel free to add your own design to the toes. Don't forget to notch and trim as necessary (see figure 1V).

15. Carefully, patiently, and gently, turn your creature right side out through the hole in its head. Start by feeding the toes through the head hole first, and let the rest of your creature follow suit.

Stuff your creature through the hole in its head (see figure 1W). Close up the hole with the closing stitch found on page 16.

Once you've mastered these instructions, invent some variations. Try different fabrics like upholstery or tea towels. Use frillier blouses for a girlish set of twins.

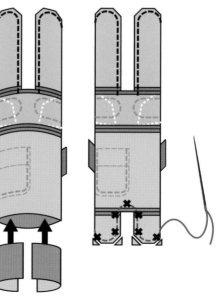

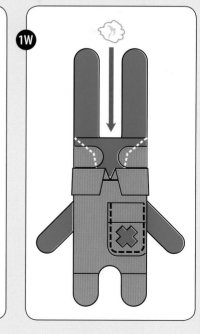

> Never force twins to hold hands. It activates our powers...

Lurwin Obsgarde

Lurwin Fossipher Obsgarde—a certified forester—spends his time hard at work clearing fallen timbers. He's happiest when left on his own to work the live-long day. On weekends, Lurwin visits the Leftover Lounge (his favorite diner) where he tries his best to attract the attention of the lovely waitress Camilla Grace on page 80. She's a chatterbox and he's quite soft spoken. You know what they say: opposites attract.

{ *This thick and sturdy, buffalo plaid jacket is a working man's coat designed to guard against low temperatures when the going is tough outdoors.* }

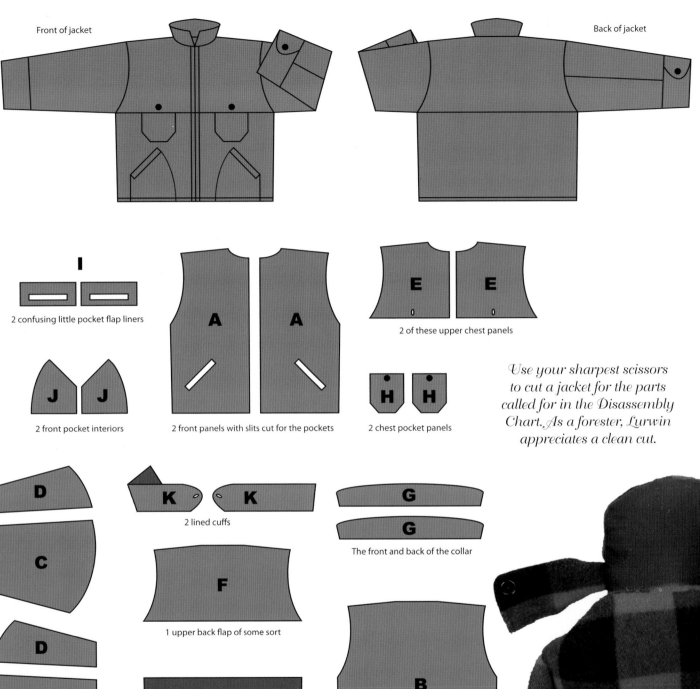

Front of jacket

Back of jacket

I

2 confusing little pocket flap liners

J J

2 front pocket interiors

A A

2 front panels with slits cut for the pockets

E E

2 of these upper chest panels

H H

2 chest pocket panels

Use your sharpest scissors to cut a jacket for the parts called for in the Disassembly Chart. As a forester, Lurwin appreciates a clean cut.

D

C

D

C

2 narrow and 2 wide sleeve panels

K K

2 lined cuffs

F

1 upper back flap of some sort

L

1 piece of lining from the back of the jacket

G

G

The front and back of the collar

B

1 back of the jacket

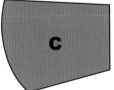

1. To cut the front and back of the body, trim part B till it's squared off. Then cut it in half to make two rectangles. Arrange the rectangles vertically with right sides facing. Round off the top edge to form the shoulders, then divide the bottom edge into two, stubby, rounded legs (see figures 2A and 2B).

2. For the arms, cut long, trapezoidal wedges from your jacket parts. Part D from the sleeves was almost perfect the way it was. All I did was trim the tops and bottoms till they were flat (see figure 2C).

3. To make the head and hands, start by folding a large piece of lining in half. From the folded lining, cut a triangle shape for the palms of your monster's hands. Cut a head shape as large as you can, or as large as you want, from the lining. Leave the bottom edge of your head shapes flat. From the remaining lining fabric, cut something to appliqué onto Lurwin's front. I cut a Valentine heart from the folded edge of the lining (see figures 2D and 2E).

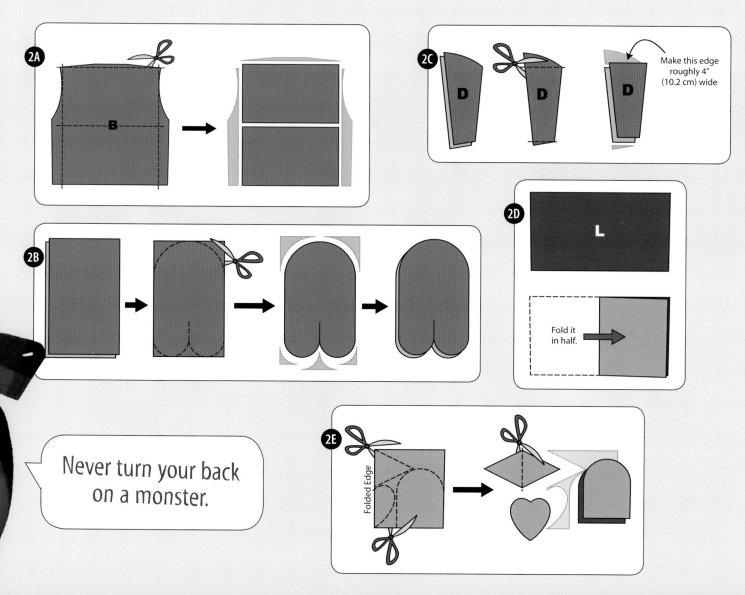

Never turn your back on a monster.

4. Find two pieces of exterior fabric large enough to fit one of the head shapes. Align them with right sides facing. Lay one of the head shapes atop the fabric, and trace its top edge and about one-third of its length. Set the head shape aside and draw a bulbous, wide nose onto the line you traced. Cut out the shapes and set them aside (see figure 2F).

5. We'll leave the sleeve cuffs as they are for his ears, and we'll attach an existing pocket to his back just because it's there and it's a shame not to use it (see figure 2G).

6. By now you've cut all of Lurwin's parts. You should have all the parts (and them some) needed for Lurwin: front and back of the body, two palms, two arms, front and back of the head, front and back of the forehead and nose, two pocket flaps for ears, and a pocket. Use your leftover fabric for any appliqué shapes you want (see figure 2H).

Stitching

7. Now that you've thoroughly destroyed a perfectly good jacket, here's how we're going to reassemble at least part of it into a monster. However, first, go ahead and add any appliqué you wish and stitch the pocket onto Lurwin's back (see figure 2I).

8. Use the Gusseted Palm arm method, found on page 18, to make Lurwin's arms (see figure 2J). Stuff the arms, and leave ½ inch (1.3 cm) of empty space at their open ends. If you want to add beanbag fill, add it to the very tips of the fingers before you put any stuffing in. Then stuff as normal.

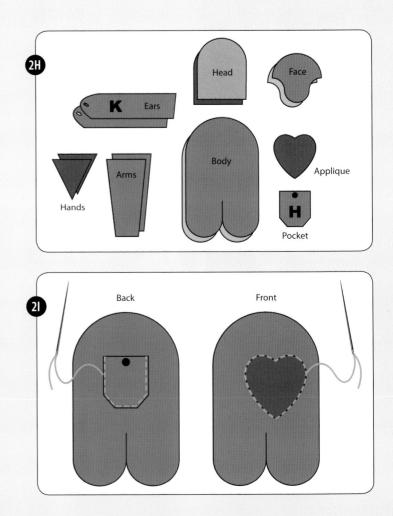

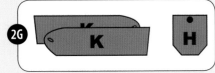

9. Arrange the parts you cut for his face with right sides facing and stitch their nose edges together. Leave the curve of the crown open. Turn the face right side out. Add a scoop or two of beanbag fill to the nose and shake it all down to settle it (see figures 2K and 2L).

10. Lay the face atop the front of Lurwin's head. Align the top edges (the crown) to match and pin into place. Top-stitch the face onto the head to add detail and hold the face in place (see figure 2M).

11. Grab one of the sleeve cuffs you've reserved for the ears and lay it right side up as shown. Fold the corners of the bottom edge in towards the middle of the ear and pin into place. If your sleeve cuff still has a button on it, now's the time to get rid of it (see figure 2N).

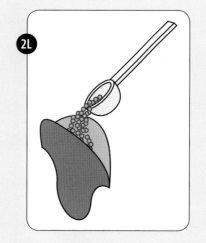

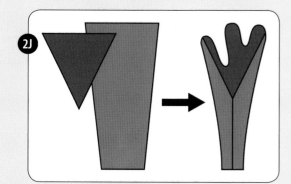

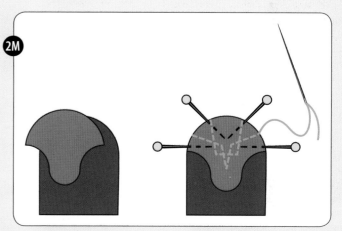

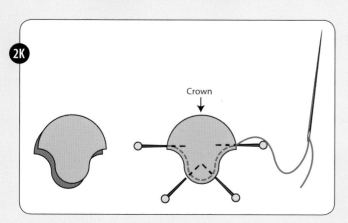

Crown

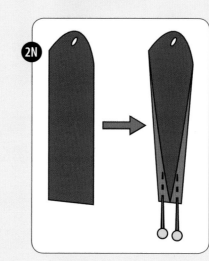

12. Attach the back of Lurwin's head to the front of his body using the Bubble Method found on page 32. Insert the ears between the two layers of Lurwin's face. Make sure the front of the ear touches the front of the face. If the ears are longer than the width of the face, you can poke the ears through the neck hole so you don't stitch in the loose end by mistake. Stitch the front and the back of Lurwin's head together, clamping the ears into place. Give Lurwin's head a toothy edge by stitching rectangular shapes across its width (see figures 2O, 2P, and 2Q). Don't you love making heads?

13. Snip the seam allowance between Lurwin's teeth to separate them. Notch the corners between the teeth, and trim their bottom corners (see figure 2R).

14. Place the arms—palms down—atop the front of Lurwin's body. Match the open ends to the edges of his body. Lay the back of Lurwin's body atop his front and hands with right sides facing. Stitch around the edges leaving enough seam allowance to suit the fabric you're using. Leave a space unstitched at the top for turning and stuffing (see figures 2S and 2T).

15. Turn Lurwin right side out. Stuff him and close him up with a closing stitch found on page 16. Finish Lurwin's look by sewing some buttons on where you want his eyes to go (see figures 2U and 2V).

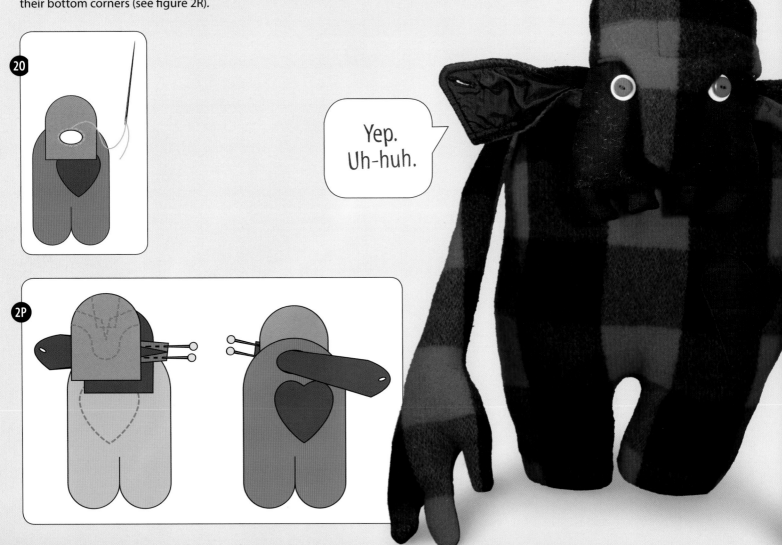

Yep.
Uh-huh.

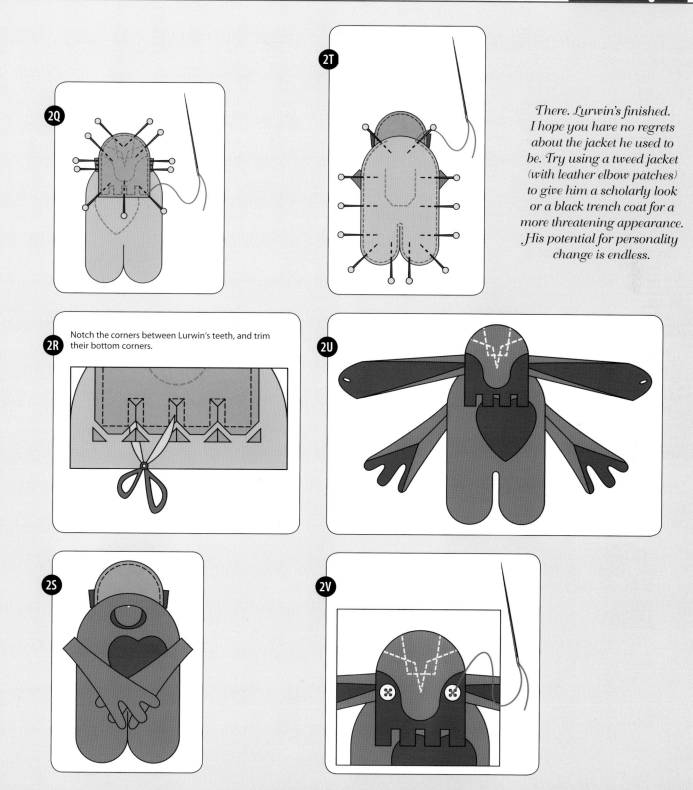

2Q

2T

There, Lurwin's finished.
I hope you have no regrets
about the jacket he used to
be. Try using a tweed jacket
(with leather elbow patches)
to give him a scholarly look
or a black trench coat for a
more threatening appearance.
His potential for personality
change is endless.

2R Notch the corners between Lurwin's teeth, and trim their bottom corners.

2U

2S

2V

Wazman Standers

Wazman Standers is a runty, nervous kid who reads too many comic books and chooses to bask in the glow of his computer screen rather than go outside. His parents can rarely coax Wazman into going sailing with them, but they sometimes succeed with extreme duress and the blanketing daze of motion sickness pills. Frankly, Wazman might benefit from some sunshine and sea spray if he'd give it a chance.

{ *The sturdy fabric and decorative excess of these ladies' slacks remind me of something someone's mother might wear to the marina for cocktails in the lounge or for a brief run around the bay.* }

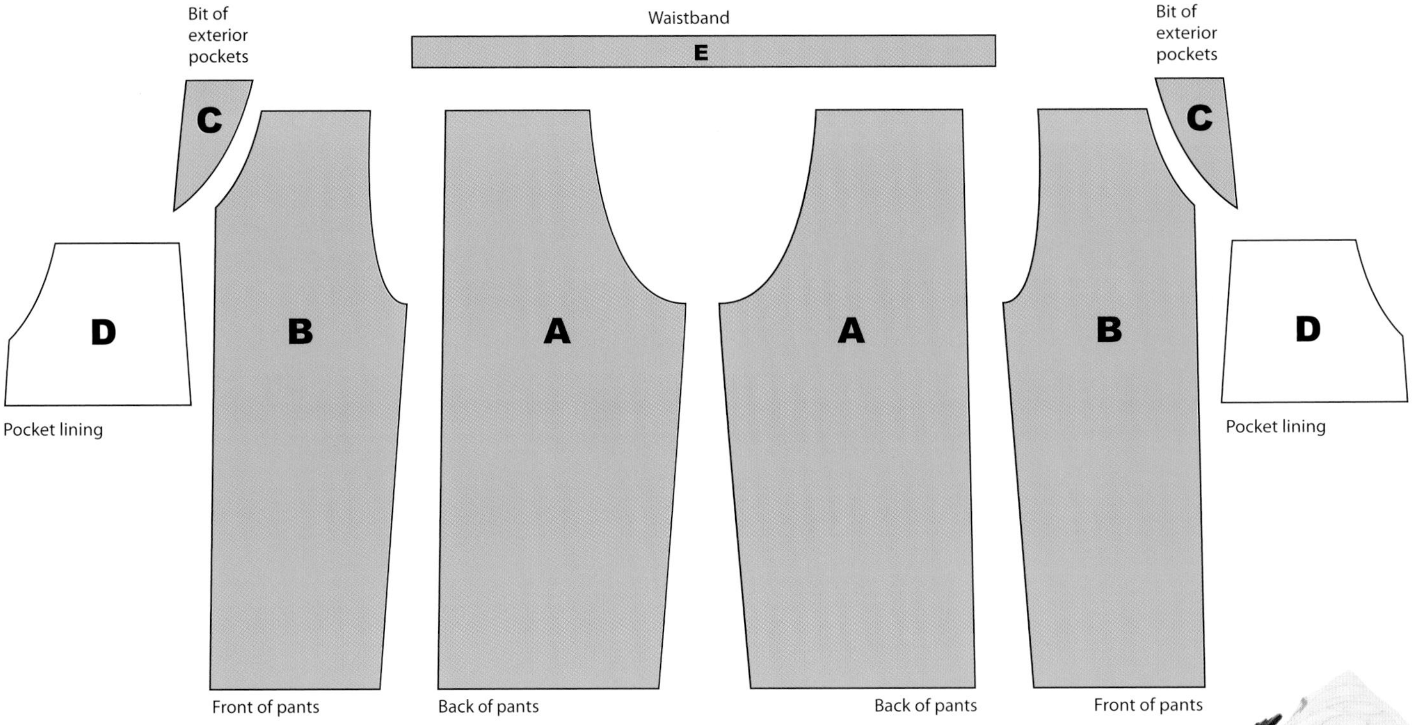

Bit of exterior pockets

C

Waistband

E

Bit of exterior pockets

C

D

Pocket lining

B

Front of pants

A

Back of pants

A

Back of pants

B

Front of pants

D

Pocket lining

Dismantle a pair of trousers, slacks, or capri pants for Wazman, as shown in the Disassembly Chart.

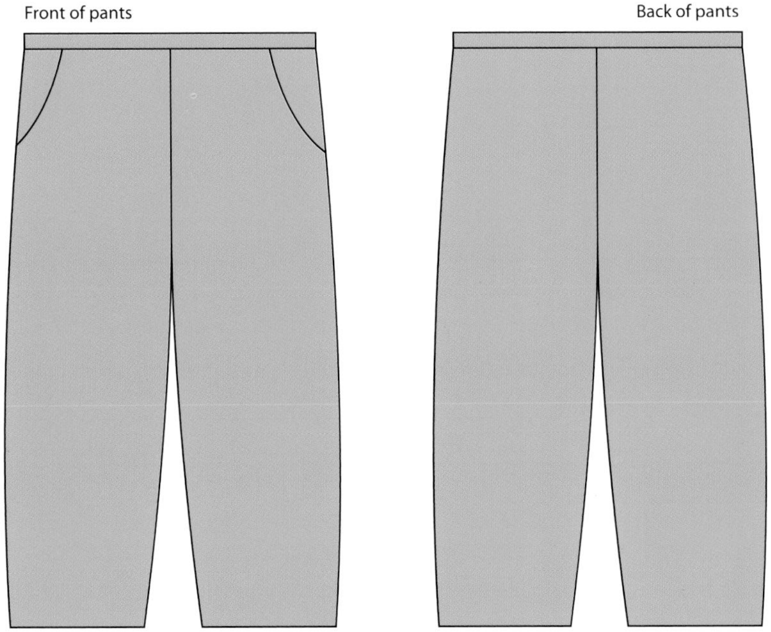

Front of pants

Back of pants

Can somebody pop my back?

1. Arrange parts B from the pants together with right sides facing. We're going to cut Wazman's body and head from this. Decide how long a torso you want, and cut the pants horizontally there. Then, decide how big you want Wazman's face to be and make another horizontal cut (see figure 3A).

2. Arrange the fronts and backs of your body and head together with opposite sides facing up. Stitch the pieces back together with the right side of the body touching the wrong

side of the head. Leave about 4 inches (10 cm) unsewn in the middle of the back of the body for a stuffing hole (see figures 3B and 3C).

3. Unfold the front and back of your creature and press the seams. Arrange them with right sides facing (bear in mind, the wrong side of the fabric is now the right side of the face), and stitch them together at their top edge (see figure 3D).

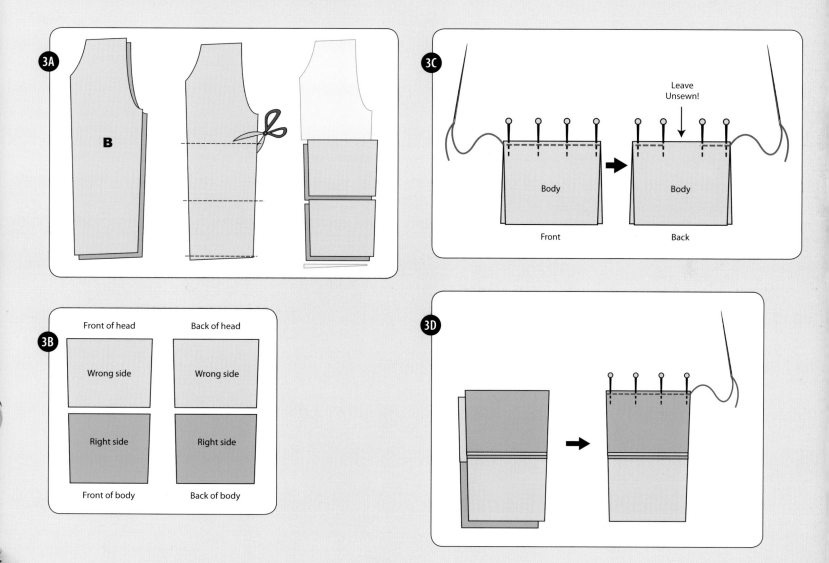

3A

B

3C

Leave Unsewn!

Body

Body

Front

Back

3B

Front of head   Back of head

Wrong side   Wrong side

Right side   Right side

Front of body   Back of body

3D

4. Unfold the body and press the seam you just stitched. Now's the time to put on any decorative topstitching you may want to include. Be sure not to stitch over your stuffing hole. When you've done all the topstitching you want, cut a horizontal line across Wazman's face where you want his mouth to go (see figures 3E and 3F).

5. Cut a long rectangle of fabric that's the same width and combined height of the front and back of your creature. Use lighter fabric than pants material for this rectangle. Consider leftovers from Flapp and Cuff (page 36) (see figure 3G).

6. Use the Gusseted Palm method on page 18 to cut parts for arms and hands. Use scrap material like the leftovers from part B (see figure 3H).

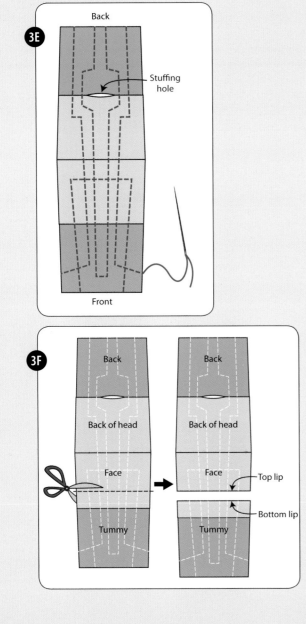

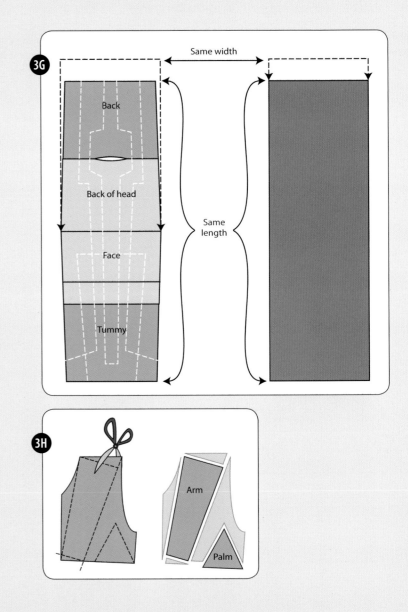

7. Cut eye appliqué shapes and ears from pants remnants if they're big enough and can yield the shape you want. Otherwise, cut these shapes from another part of the pants. I used the premade shapes from the pockets and pocket linings for Wazman's ears. To do this, I traced a part C onto a part D with a fabric pen and cut along that line to make the ear's lining. Finish the ears by snipping their corners. We'll use that edge for turning the ears right side out after we've sewn them together (see figures 3I, 3J, 3K, and 3L).

8. Use the remainder of the pocket lining (part D) to cut parts for Wazman's teeth. Use the tooth-making instructions on page 27 (see figure 3M).

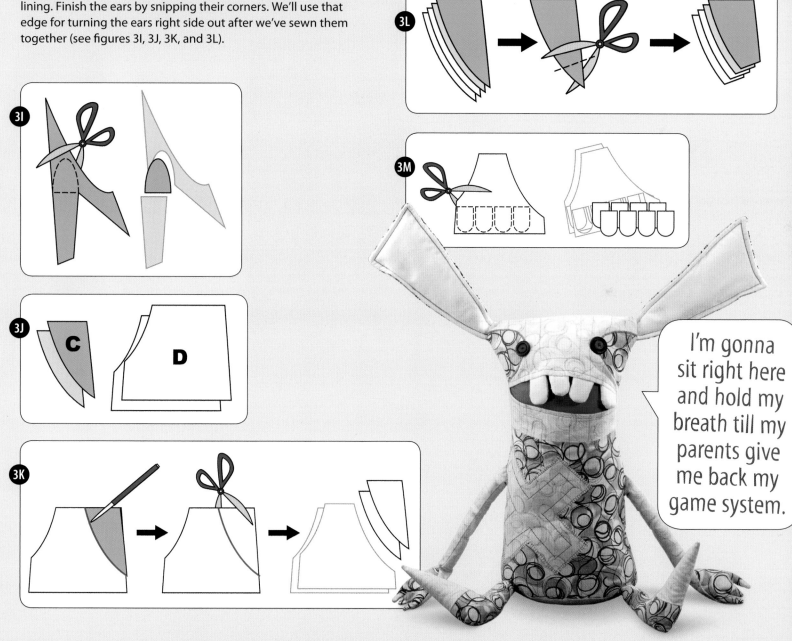

I'm gonna sit right here and hold my breath till my parents give me back my game system.

9. Cut the parts for Wazman's legs and feet using parts A. Cut a long, 3- or 4-inch-wide (7.6 or 10 cm) strip from its entire length, then cut that horizontally into two equal parts. Cut a big oval (approximately 5 x 8 inches [12.7 x 20 cm]) for the feet, and divide it in half horizontally.

Measure the bottom edges of Wazman's body and calculate how big a circle you'll need for his butt. Cut that out, too. Use the Creature Feature Bottoms instructions on page 28 to calculate the size of Wazman's butt (see figure 3N).

10. Check out figure 3O to see an overview of the parts you should have prepared for Wazman.

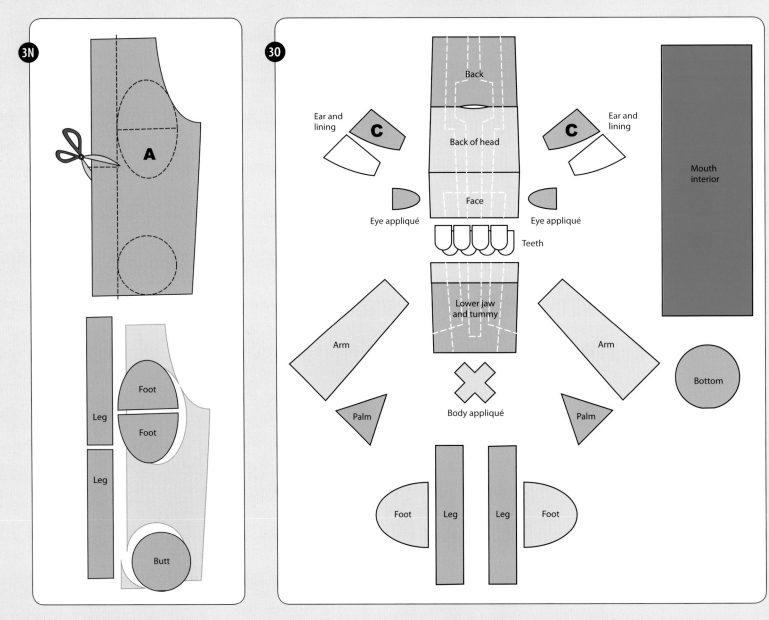

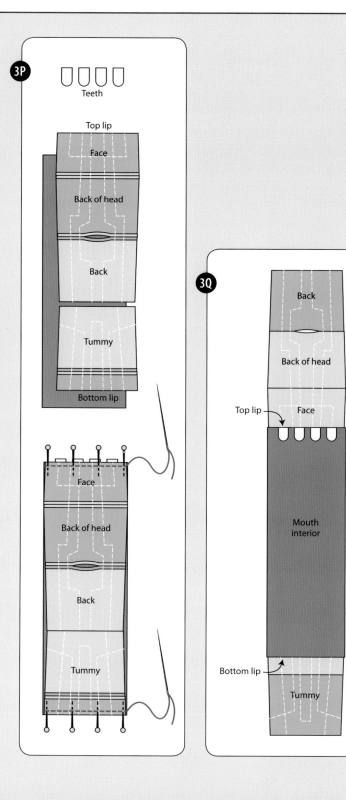

Stitching

11.   Lay the mouth interior flat. Turn Wazman's body pieces upside down, and then flip them wrong side up. Lay those parts atop the mouth interior as shown. Insert the teeth between the top lip and the mouth interior. Stitch those edges together, clamping the teeth into place. Stitch the edge of the bottom lip to the bottom edge of the mouth interior. Unfold what you've sewn and press the seams. Lay the whole thing flat (see figures 3P and 3Q).

12.   Bring the top lip down towards the bottom lip. Fold the mouth interior so that it rests in kind of a big loop behind the face and front of the body (see figure 3R).

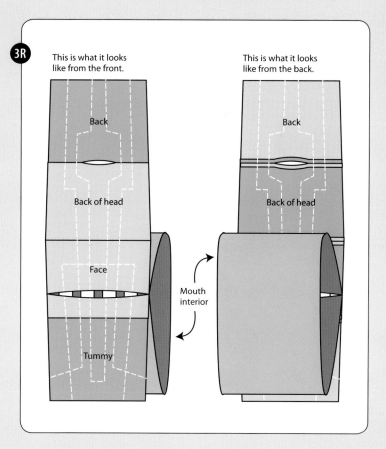

13. Press the folds at the edges of the lips and sew a seam about ³⁄₈ inch (.95 cm) away from their edges to stabilize the fold. Place pins where the mouth interior meets the head seam and where it meets the bottom edge of Wazman's body. Appliqué the eye patches to Wazman's face. Let the appliqué stitches go through the mouth interior that touches the back of the face. This will hold the mouth interior in place. Turn the whole thing over and sew the appliqué to the body. Sew through the layer of mouth interior it touches so that all layers are held in place (see figures 3S, 3T, and 3U).

14. Bring the edges of the lips together and pin them in place. Flatten the mouth interior against the face and front of the body and pin all layers into place (see figure 3V).

15. Follow the Serendipitous Ear instructions on page 25 to make the ears. Use the Gusseted Palm instructions on page 18 to make the arms and stuff them. And find instructions for The Dangly Leg with a Different Colored Toe and No Sole on page 22 to make the legs (see figure 3W).

16. Fold Wazman's back down over his front with right sides touching. Pin the seams where his head meets his body. Pin the corners of his bottom edges, too. Insert the ears and arms inside Wazman between the two layers of his body. Make sure the front of the ears touch the face, and that the palms of his hands touch the front of Wazman's body. Stitch the side edges closed, sewing through both layers of the body as well as the mouth interior (see figures 3X and 3Y).

17. Insert the legs into Wazman's body. Match the open ends of the legs to the edge of the front side of the body. Let the toes point towards the front of the body. Pin the legs into place. Follow the Creature Feature Bottoms instructions on page 28 to attach Wazman's butt to his body. Stitching his bottom on will clamp the legs in place (see figure 3Z).

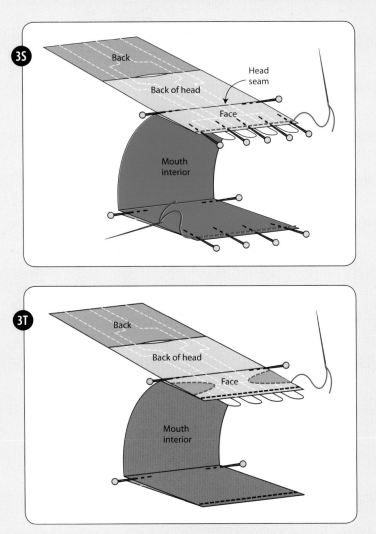

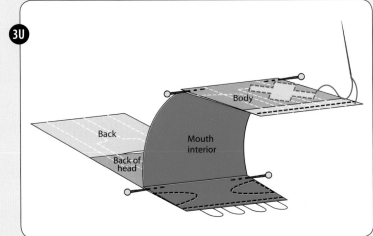

At this point, I've run out of letters of the alphabet for labeling any more diagrams. I'm going to trust you know how to turn something right side out. Take special care doing this because you've got a lot going on inside of Wazman (arms, legs, and ears, each stuffed and taking up room within him). Get his legs out first through the stuffing hole in his back, then shimmy his bottom right side out. Then get his arms out through the hole. Do this with utmost patience and care. You don't want to pop any seams. When you've got Wazman right side out, all you need to stuff is his body cavity (which includes his big, empty head). Stuff him as firmly as you like, then close up his stuffing hole with the closing stitch found on page 16 of this book.

For such a simple looking creature,
Wazman was an adventure to put together,
wasn't he? But he's worth it. Experiment
with a t-shirt for a stretchy version of
Wazman. Use corduroys or blue jeans for
other interesting variations.

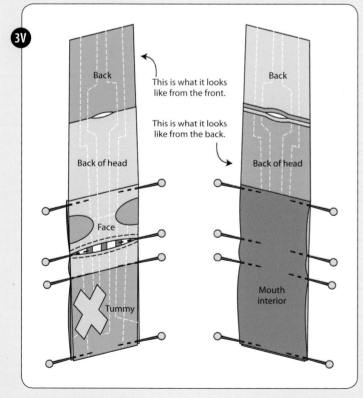

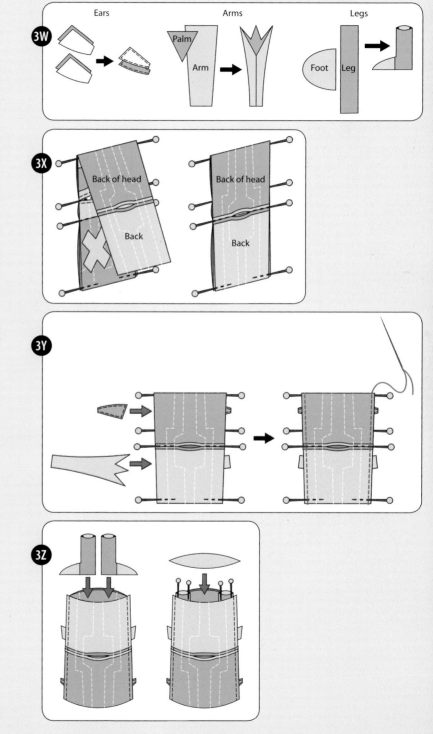

Gilmor Oothby

Gilmor Oothby is a curmudgeon. He feels that disruptions follow him like the plague; his newspapers, slippers, and keys are often lost. He once found his pills in the microwave and the cordless phone in the dryer! Senility, of course, is out of the question. It's always the fault of communists, those young 'uns, or Ronny, that wastrel grandson of his. He feels safest at the Leftover Lounge, where he occupies an entire booth for eight solid hours, complaining about everything he sees.

Sometimes the character a garment suggests has nothing to do with its function or color. This sweater's floppy turtleneck looked like a grumbling, fretful mouth, so I built a creature to fit.

Prepare to make Gilmor by disassembling a pullover shirt or sweater as shown in the Disassembly Chart. (Cut his parts carefully or you'll never hear the end of it!)

What?! Cut up a perfectly good sweater? Folks these days don't know what a good sweater's worth.

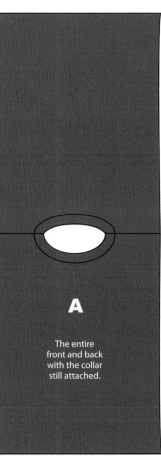

A

The entire front and back with the collar still attached.

B

Sleeve

B

Sleeve

1. Lay part A, the torso, flat. Snip off half the length of the torso above and below the collar. This will establish how tall Gilmor will be (see figure 4A).

2. To cut the contours for Gilmor's head, fold the collared portion of part A in half vertically and lay flat as shown. Decide the profile you'd like Gilmor to have, and round off the upper corners accordingly. Set this part aside (see figure 4B).

3. Using the Gusseted Palm instructions from page 18, cut parts for two arms and two palms from one of the sleeves (part B). Trim the shoulder off, and cut it into palms. Divide the rest of the sleeve into vertical halves (see figure 4C).

4. Use the shoulder of the other sleeve to cut Gilmor's bottom. Measure the bottom edge of Gilmor's body from step 1. That measurement will be the perimeter of Gilmor's bottom. Follow the Creature Feature Bottoms instructions on page 28 to use that measurement to draw a circle or oval of the right size. Cut the remaining part of the sleeve into vertical halves to make the ears (see figure 4D).

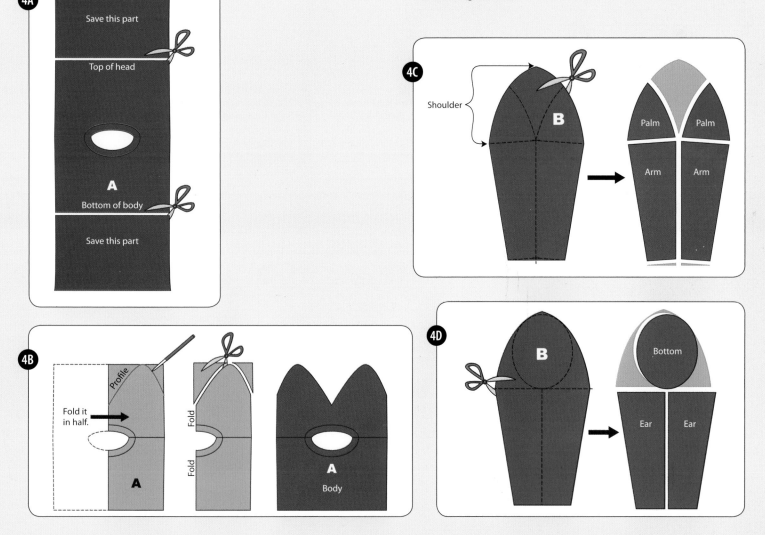

5. Use one of the remnants from part A to make the legs. Just cut it in half, as shown, for now. We'll turn them into legs when it's time to sew (see figure 4E).

6. Find a remnant of dark or black fabric to use for the inside of Gilmor's mouth. Cut an oval that overlaps the seam of the collar by a good inch (2.5 cm) all the way around (see figure 4F).

7. Grab the other remnant from part A and cut off the top 6 inches (15 cm) or so. We'll use this part to make the ridge of spikes down Gilmor's back (see figure 4G).

8. Use remnants from other projects (or this one if you have enough) to cut bottoms for Gilmor's feet, eye patches and teeth. Find instructions for making teeth on page 27, and use the Creature Feature Bottoms instructions on page 28 to cut the right-size foot bottoms for Gilmor (see figure 4H).

Make sure you've cut everything you need for Gilmor or he'll roar at you as you stitch (figure 4I).

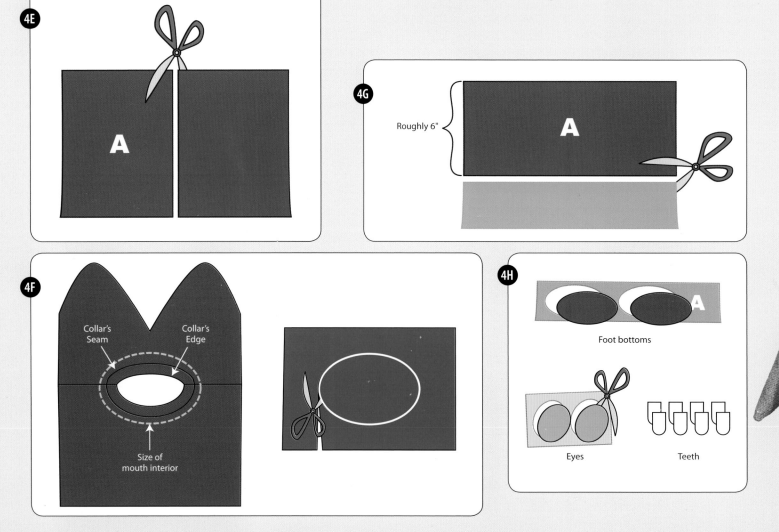

4E

4G

Roughly 6"

A

4F

Collar's Seam

Collar's Edge

Size of mouth interior

4H

A

Foot bottoms

Eyes

Teeth

4I

Ear

Spine ridge

Ear

Teeth

Eyes

Body

Palm

Palm

Arm

Arm

Leg

Leg

Foot bottom

Foot bottom

Bottom

In my day, sweaters were called knitty shirts, and we wore those instead of long johns, which were called squatty pants…

Stitching

9.   Let's make the spiny ridge for Gilmor's back first. Use the section you cut from part A in step 7 to do this. Fold it in half, matching wide edge to wide edge with right sides touching. Lay the folded piece atop a layer of batting or soft fleece. Do not put this padding in between the folded layers. Next, draw a series of wide triangles or bumps to define the ridges. The ridges should point towards the fold of the fabric. Stitch about ⅜ inch (.95 cm) beneath the line you drew, and sew the side edges closed. Snip away the excess fabric between the ridges, making sure to notch their valleys and trim their peaks. Turn the ridges right side out, trapping the padding inside. Stitch a seam about ⅜ inch (.95 cm) in from the edge of the ridges to stabilize the shape. And that's that (see figures 4J, 4K, and 4L).

10.   Grab the parts you cut for Gilmor's hands and arms and assemble them using the Gusseted Palm instructions on page 18. Grab the parts you cut to make the legs and their bottoms, and follow the Basic Dangly Leg instructions on page 21 to put them all together. Stuff the legs, but leave ½ inch (1.3 cm) of unstuffed space at the opening (see figures 4M and 4N).

11.   To make Gilmor's ears, grab one of the ear pieces you cut, and fold it in half vertically. Stitch the long edges together leaving adequate seam allowance for the fabric you're using. Flatten the resulting tube with the seam in the middle and facing you. Stitch a V shape below the top edge and trim the excess material. Don't forget to notch and trim! Turn the ear wrong side out (see figures 4O and 4P).

12.   Appliqué Gilmor's eye spots where you think they ought to go. See the appliqué instructions on page 38 (see figure 4Q).

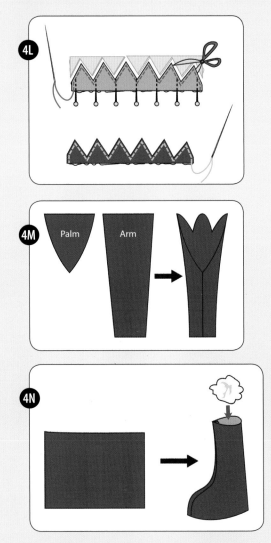

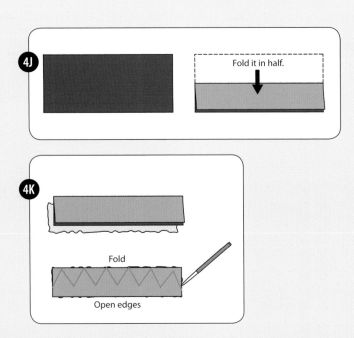

13. Flip the body wrong side up and arrange the teeth around the collar where you want them to go. Make sure the open ends of the teeth overlap the collar's seam. Lay the mouth interior atop the collar, wrong side down. It should overlap the collar seam entirely. Pin it into place. Take care not to let the teeth shift. Flip the body right side up and stitch the mouth and teeth into place by sewing right along the collar's seam. Be sure the teeth don't shift as you do this (see figures 4R, 4S, and 4T).

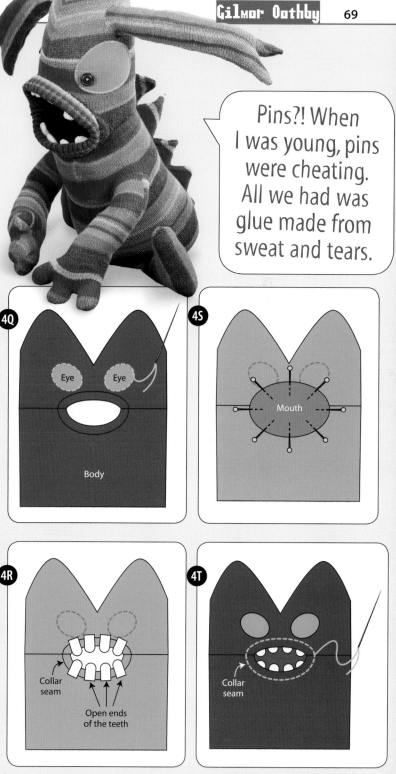

Pins?! When I was young, pins were cheating. All we had was glue made from sweat and tears.

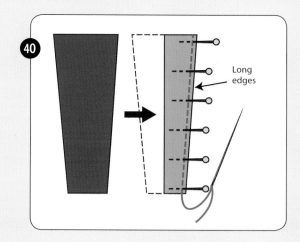

40

Long edges

4P

4Q

Eye   Eye

Body

4S

Mouth

4R

Collar seam

Open ends of the teeth

4T

Collar seam

14. Fold the body in half vertically with right sides touching. Insert the ridges, pointy side first, in between the two layers of the body. Align the open edge of the ridges with the open edges of the body. Stitch Gilmor shut around his head and down his back. Leave at least a ³⁄₈-inch (.95 cm) seam allowance (see figures 4U and 4V).

15. Use the Circumference method instructions on page 31 to attach Gilmor's ears and arms (see figure 4W).

16. Insert the legs into the body with the toes touching the front of the body. Secure them there with pins. Attach Gilmor's bottom using the Creature Bottom instructions on page 28. This will clamp the legs into place. Leave a good 4 inches (10 cm) of butt circumference unstitched so you can turn Gilmor right side out and stuff him.

17. Stuff Gilmor through the hole you left unstitched in his butt. Feel free to first add beanbag fill to his ears and hands. See page 17 for tips on beanbag fill and for tips on stuffing. Close up Gilmor's stuffing hole using the closing stitch found on page 16.

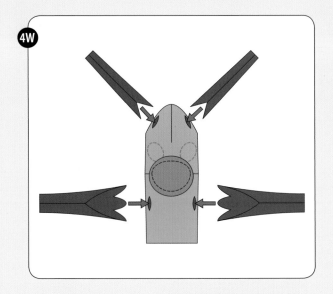

And that's Gilmor in a nutshell. Disassemble a sweatshirt with a nicely pilled interior for your next attempt. A long sleeved t-shirt will bring life to a stretchier version of Gilmor.

What you need, boy, is a job. A job and a wife and…

Ronny Oothby

Ronny Oothby bears a resemblance to his grandfather, but certainly hasn't developed his work ethic. Ronny likes to spend entire days with his entourage, sipping expensive lattés at the Leftover Lounge, where they wax on about the state of the world and its many (many!) imperfections. He certainly has his grandpa's propensity to complain!

{ *To make Ronny Oothby, you'll follow the instructions for his grandfather, Gilmor, on pages 62–70 almost to the letter, but with the following course corrections.* }

1. Skip step 2 of Gilmor's instructions entirely. We won't be contouring Ronny's head.

2. When you reach step 4, don't make any ears. Just like Ronny, we're avoiding work!

3. Avoid step 11 as though it's a major responsibility. Continue with Gilmor's instructions.

4. Proceed with step 14, arranging and sewing the spinal ridges the same way you'd do with Gilmor, but only stitch down Ronny's back. There are no head contours to sew shut (see figures 4U and 4V on page 70).

5. Arrange Ronny's body tube wrong side out and mouth side up. Keep the spinal seam in the very middle. Draw two bumpy ears at the top of his head where you think they ought to go. Cut along the line you drew, then pin and sew the layers shut. Remember to notch between the ears so they'll turn out right (see figure 4X).

6. Resume Gilmor's instructions at step 15 to attach the arms, and follow the instructions as written until Ronny is done.

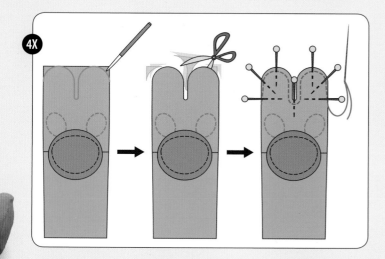

4X

Ulee Bingham

Ulee Bingham comes from another planet, representing an off-world conglomerate of property developers seeking new territory on Earth. Unexpectedly, Ulee became quite attached to his new home, and has since been dodging his alien supervisor's questions on his progress of annexing this planet. He met his truest friend on earth—the reclusive, sci-fi junkie Wazman Standers—online, of course.

{ *I'm a big fan of sweatshirts because they have obviously right and wrong sides. The wrong side of fabric, if its color and texture is appealing, often adds contrast and dimension to a monster. We'll take advantage of the under-sung "wrong" side and use it as the right side for Ulee.* }

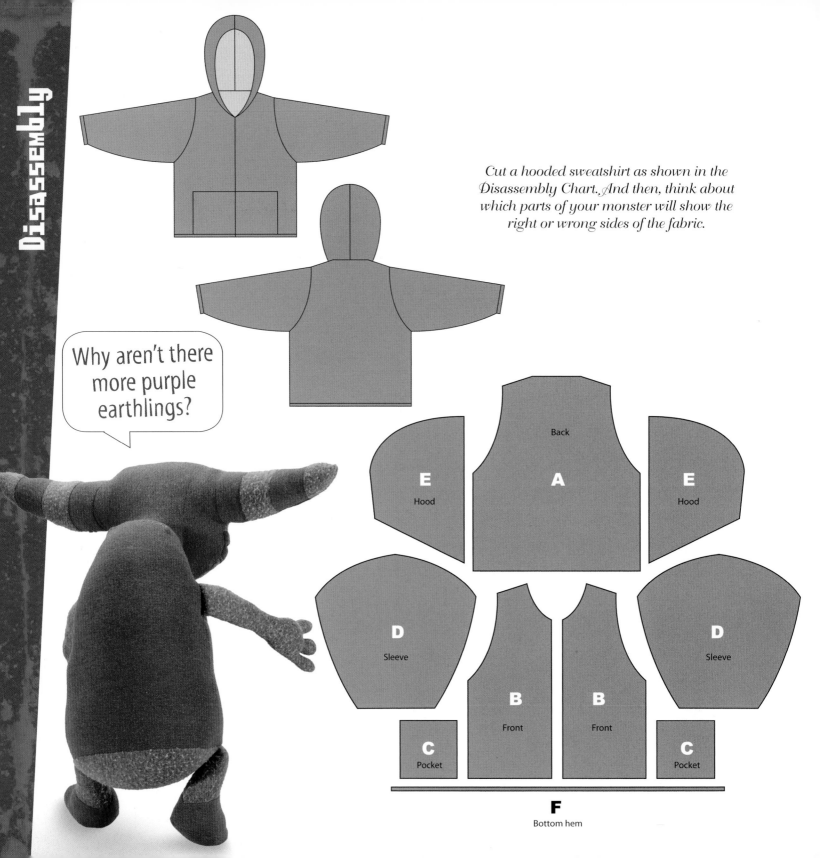

Cut a hooded sweatshirt as shown in the Disassembly Chart. And then, think about which parts of your monster will show the right or wrong sides of the fabric.

Why aren't there more purple earthlings?

E Hood

A Back

E Hood

D Sleeve

B Front

B Front

D Sleeve

C Pocket

C Pocket

F Bottom hem

1. Align parts B together with wrong sides facing. Match up all the edges and curves. Cut off the shoulder portion of the pieces as shown, and trim them so they're rounded at the top and reasonably symmetrical. Split the stomach portion horizontally into halves. One set of halves will become Ulee's legs. The other set will be used for foot bottoms and appliqué pieces (see figure 5A).

2. To cut parts for Ulee's arms, grab one of the sleeves. Fold it in half vertically. Then fold it in half again. Decide how long you want Ulee's arms to be and cut a length of the sleeve off accordingly. Trim the arm parts to make them symmetrical and cut along the folded edges to separate them (see figures 5B and 5C).

3. To cut Ulee's legs out, use one of the stomach portion halves you cut in step 1 and fold it in half with right sides touching. Cut the folded piece diagonally into halves. Arrange the parts with different sides up. We will make dangly legs that look like shoes out of these pieces (see figure 5D).

4. Align both parts C together and round their corners. These parts will be the front and back of Ulee's head (see figure 5E).

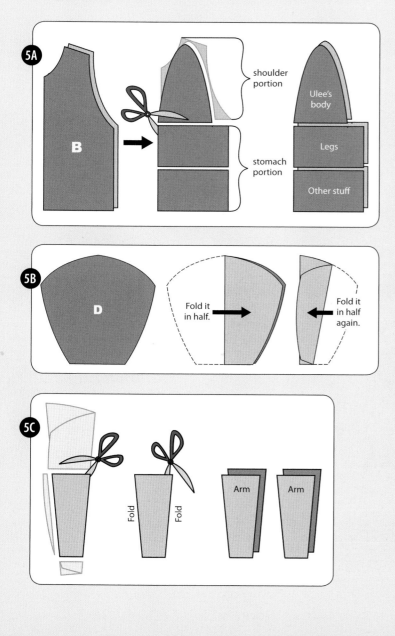

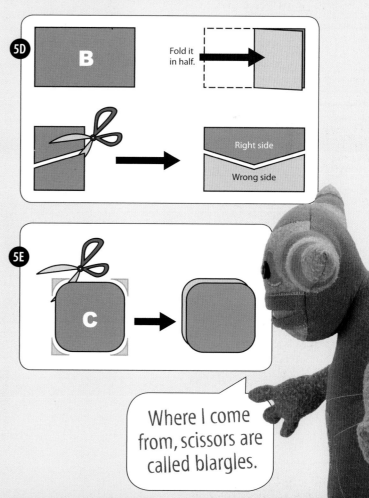

Where I come from, scissors are called blargles.

5. Use one of the hood halves, part E, to cut the parts for Ulee's ears. Fold it in half using the front edge as a base. Trim the part into a tall trapezoid that's reasonably symmetrical. Then cut along the folded edge to separate the shapes, and divide them into four strips of even thickness (see figure 5F).

6. Trim one of the remaining stomach portions of part B into appliqué parts. You'll need two eye circles, a widow's peak for his forehead, and a star for Ulee's chest. Use the last piece of part B to cut foot bottoms. Do this when you've made Ulee's legs and calculated how big they need to be (see figure 5G).

7. Measure the bottom edge of Ulee's body and make a round bottom (page 28) from the remaining hood half (see figure 5H).

8. Trim from part F (the bottom hem of the jacket) two strips just a bit longer than the width of Ulee's face. These will be his lips (see figure 5I).

Refer to figure 5J to see that you've got all the parts you need to assemble your alien friend.

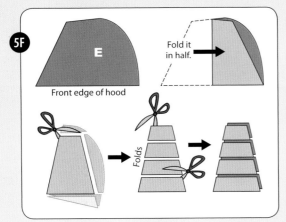

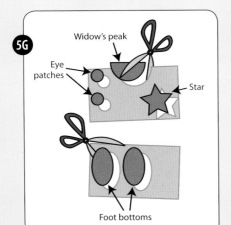

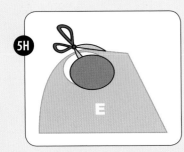

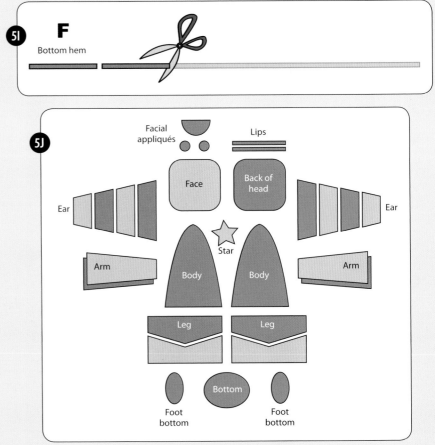

Stitching

9. Start assembling Ulee by taking care of appliqués and top-stitching. Attach the eye patches and widow's peak right side up to Ulee's face, which is wrong side up. Attach the star wrong side up to Ulee's chest, which is right side up. Add any decorative top-stitching you may want. Lay Ulee's lips where you want them to go with the folded edges touching. Attach them to his face with a zigzag or overcast stitch (see figures 5K and 5L).

10. Lay the back of Ulee's head atop the front of his body with right sides touching. Attach the head to the body using the Bubble Method found on page 32 (see figure 5M).

11. Push the back of Ulee's head through the hole where you sewed it to his body and lay it atop his face. Stitch the top edges of Ulee's head (see figure 5N). Set Ulee aside for the moment.

12. Follow the Mentacle ear instructions on page 26 to make Ulee's ears. Attach them to his head using the Arc method, found on page 30. Finish off Ulee's head by stitching shut the open edges of the ears and lower jaw. Don't forget to trim any excess from Ulee's ears (see figure 5O).

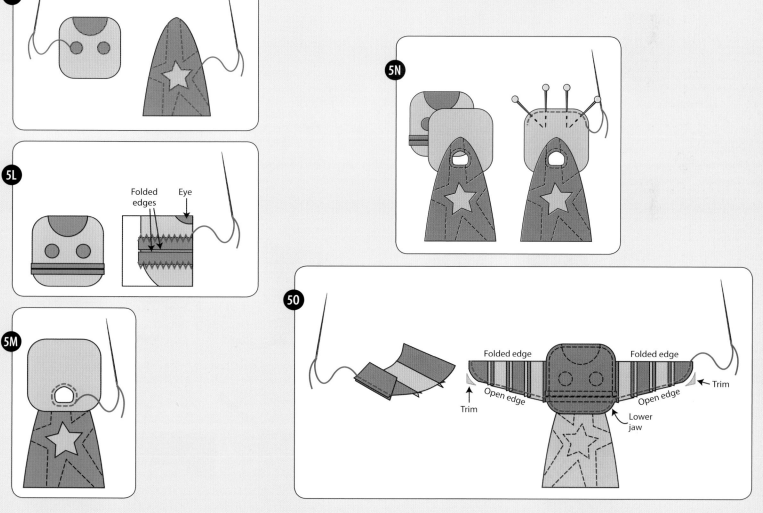

13. Arrange the parts you cut for Ulee's arms wrong sides together and follow the instructions for the Freefinger Arm on page 20. Stuff the arms, leaving ¹/₂ inch (1.3 cm) of unstuffed space at the open end (see figure 5P).

14. Lay Ulee's arms where you want them to go on the right side of his body. Align the back of Ulee's body with the front, right sides together. Pin it into place and sew around the edge. Leave a good 4 inches (10 cm) unstitched at the top of the body for turning and stuffing, and leave the bottom unsewn (see figure 5Q).

15. Grab the pieces you cut for Ulee's legs. Make sure the upper part is right side up and the lower part is wrong side up. Sew them back together at the angled edge where you cut it. It's a bit tricky for the purpose of diagramming, but it's really not that hard. Open the sewn pieces back up and flatten them out. Press the seam if it helps the piece lie flatter. Fold the piece in half matching the short sides. Keep the seam allowances on the outside. Draw the shape of a leg and foot onto the piece with the toe pointing away from the fold. Stitch along the line you drew and trim the excess. Attach the foot bottoms to Ulee's legs using the Creature Feature Bottoms instructions on page 28 (see figures 5R, 5S, and 5T). Stuff the legs, leaving ¹/₂ inch (1.3 cm) of unstuffed space at the open end.

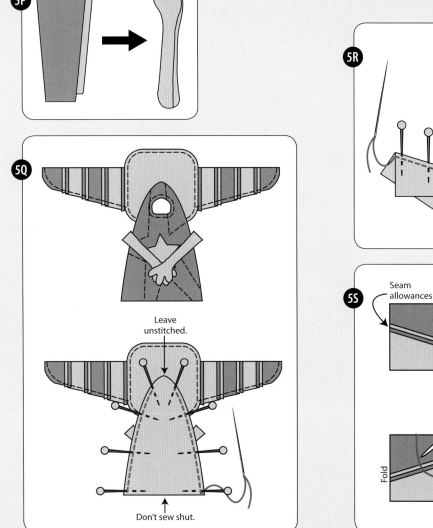

16. With the legs right side out and the body wrong side out, insert the legs into the body with the toes touching the front of the body. Pin them into place. Attach Ulee's bottom using the Creature Bottom instructions on page 28 (see figure 5U).

17. Now stuff Ulee through the hole in his back. Stuff his ears first, then his head, then his body (see figure 5V).

Finish Ulee off with a closing stitch. Add buttons to his eye pads to give him a beady, skeptical leer.

A waterproof raincoat would give Ulee a slick, sci-fi feel. Or bring him to life with a pleather jacket or taffeta bridesmaid's dress. There's a plethora of otherworldly fabrics for alien creations.

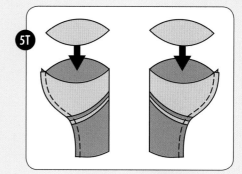

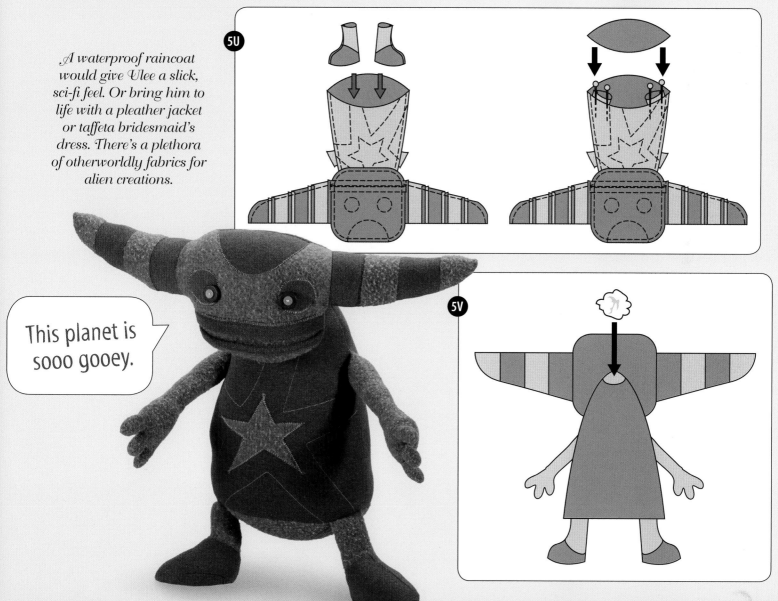

This planet is sooo gooey.

Camilla Grace

The lively Camilla Grace is many customers' favorite waitress at the Leftover Lounge. She's almost annoyingly perky and oblivious to phrases such as "No thank you, I don't want more coffee," or "Please stop singing, this is a funeral!" The quiet, stoic Lurwin Obsgarde adores her, but Camilla is blind to his silent yearning.

When I looked at the colors of these functional, but girly pajamas, I definitely saw a girl who likes to be silly from time to time. I like to think of her as a recent college graduate, working hard at her first job. At the end of the day, she loves popcorn and a movie with her upstairs neighbor, Rhodee.

Prepare to create your own Camilla by taking apart a set of flannel, silky, or cotton pajamas as shown in the Disassembly Chart.

F Collar

F

C   C

Sleeve   Front   Back   Front   Sleeve

D   B   A   B   D

E   E

Sleeve cuff G   Drawstring ribbon   Sleeve cuff

H Waistband

J   I   I   J

Front of leg   Back of leg   Back of leg   Front of leg

Leg cuff K   K Leg cuff

OMG! Pajama party!!

1. Align parts B together with right sides facing. Use a sleeve curve to guide you in drawing the profile of a torso. Think of the sleeve curve as the contour of Camilla's chest, indicating a forward-slumping posture. Draw the torso you want and cut it out, giving you the right and left halves of Camilla's body (see figure 6A).

2. Align parts J, from the pajama bottoms, together with right sides facing. Draw and cut a big egg shape out from the bottom portion of the shape. These egg shapes will be the top and bottom of Camilla's head. Keeping thrift a priority, use the remainder of parts J to divide into parts for legs and arms. You will want two blocky rectangles per limb. I cut Camilla's arms longer than her legs. You may proportion her limbs as you see fit (see figures 6B and 6C).

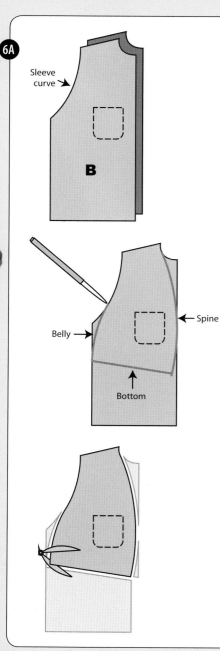

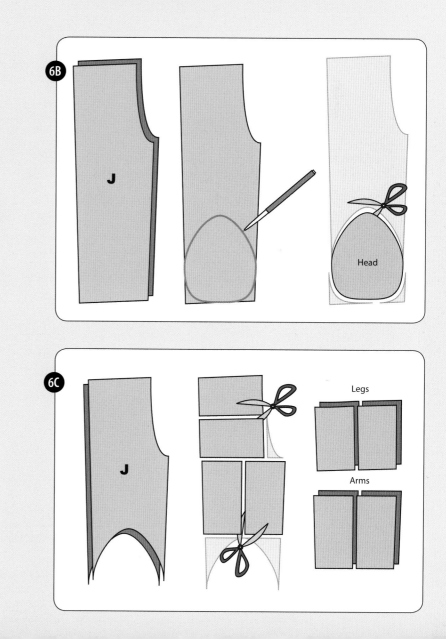

3. Trim Camilla's legs and arms into the shapes and contours you desire. Cut slits where you want her fingers and toes to be. We will give the digits more shape and definition when we get around to stitching (see figure 6D).

4. Measure the bottom edge of one of Camilla's body shapes. Follow the Creature Feature Bottom directions on page 28 to make her bottom from the remains of part B (see figure 6E).

5. We will now grab some parts and use them as they are. Use parts E for Camilla's ears. Use parts F for the ridges down her back. If your pajamas don't provide these shapes, cut suitable parts from the ample remaining pajama fabric you still ought to have. Now we'll add a piece of wow to Camilla. The pajamas I used had a silk(ish) ribbon (part G) for a drawstring. I cut it in half and devoted each half to tie around an ear (see figure 6F and 6G).

6. For Camilla's appliquéd details—lips, eyes, and a heart—use scrap fabrics or leftovers from other projects (see figure 6H). Now refer to figure 6I (on the next page) to see all the parts we've cut to make Camilla. Make sure you aren't missing anything!

6D — Leg, Arm

6E — B

6F — E / Ears, F / Back ridges

6G

6H — Lips, Eyes, Heart

Big hearts, small hearts... I just love them all.

Stitching

7. Start Camilla's assembly by aligning her body pieces together with right sides touching. Stitch the front edges together. Lay Camilla's body flat with the right side up. Press the seam, and appliqué the heart to her body. While we're on the subject of appliqué, go ahead and attach Camilla's eyes and upper lip to one of the pieces you cut for her head. Appliqué the bottom lip to the other one (see figures 6J and 6K).

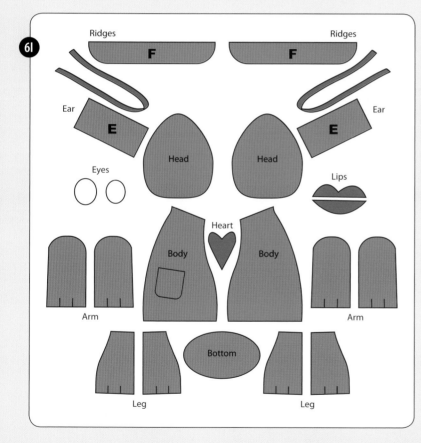

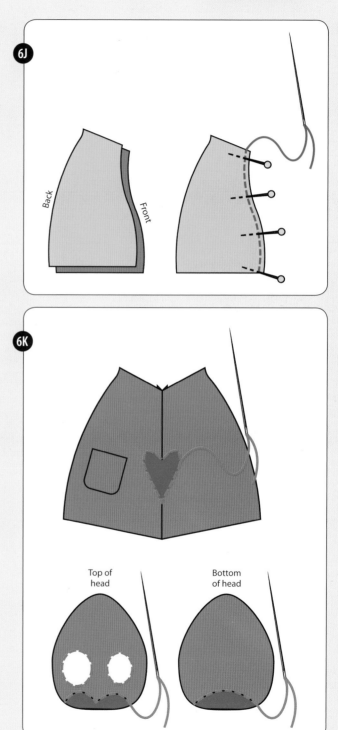

8. Use the Bubble Method found on page 32 to attach Camilla's arms. Stitch the arms shut all the way around. Don't forget to notch the spaces between the fingers and trim the corners of the seam allowance at their tips (see figure 6L).

9. To make Camilla's spinal ridges, take both parts F and align them with right sides touching. Lay them atop a piece of padding or batting that's cut to the same size and shape. Draw a series of ridges along part F as shown. Stitch along the line you drew. Don't forget to notch the corners in between the ridges. Turn the ridges right side out, trapping the padding in between the layers of fabric. Stitch a seam ¼ to ⅜ inch (8.3 mm to .95 cm) away from the edge to stabilize the piece. Insert the ridges, points first, into the open edge of Camilla's back. Match the open edge of her ridges with the open edge of her back. Stitch her back shut, fixing the ridges into place (see figures 6M and 6N).

10. Measure the opening in Camilla's neck. Cut a smaller-sized circle in the bottom half of her head about ½ inch (1.3 cm) smaller (in diameter) than the neck opening. Stuff the bottom of Camilla's head into her body, with right sides

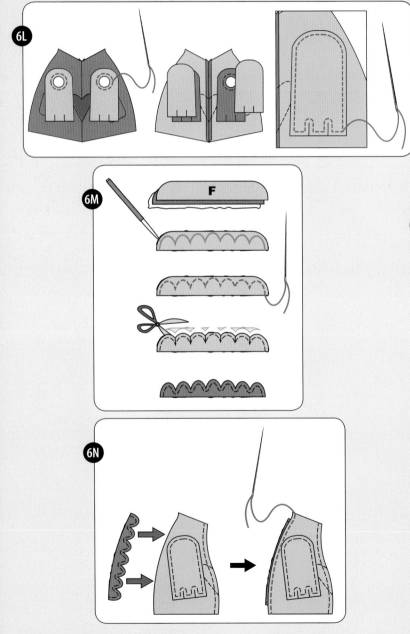

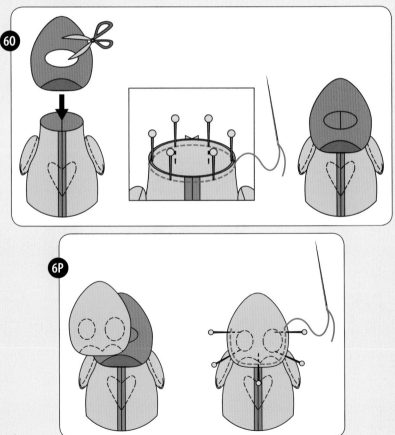

touching (I know it's a weird thing to arrange, but trust me). Make sure the bottom lip appliqué is touching the front of the body. Match the hole in Camilla's head with the opening of her neck. Stitch around the edges of the head and neck. Pull the head bottom back out of the body and lay it flat. Its right side should be up as shown. If it's not, then something's gone askew (see figure 6O).

11. Lay the top of Camilla's head atop the bottom of her head with right sides touching. Stitch the front half shut. Don't stitch the back of her head shut just yet (see figure 6P).

12. Use parts E to make long ears. Fold them in half with right sides touching, matching long edge to long edge. Attach the ears to Camilla's head using the Arc Method found on page 30. Fold the drawstring segments in half, and tuck the fold into the seam holding the ear to the head. This will allow the ribbon to dangle from the ear, or tie on like a bow. Sew shut Camilla's ears and the rest of her head. Leave $3/8$ inch (.95 cm) of seam allowance. Notch the seam allowance at the corners where Camilla's ears and head intersect (see figure 6Q).

13. Align the layers of Camilla's legs with right sides touching, and stitch them together. Remember to notch and trim her toes. Turn the legs right side out and stuff them, leaving $1/2$ inch (1.3 cm) of space unstuffed at the opening (see figure 6R).

14. Insert Camilla's feet, toe first, into her body. Pin the open ends of her legs to the front of her body. Attach her bottom using the Creature Feature Bottoms instructions on page 28. Leave a good 4 inches (10 cm) of the bottom seam unstitched in the back so you can turn Camilla right side out (see figure 6S).

15. If you want to add beanbag fill to the ends of her ears, do that first. Finish stuffing Camilla's ears first, then her head, and lastly the body. Stitch her closed with the closing stitch found on page 16.

If you don't have pajamas, a sweatsuit, long underwear, or footie pj's will do nicely. Even better: find a polyester jumpsuit from the disco era and see what it does for Camilla's personality.

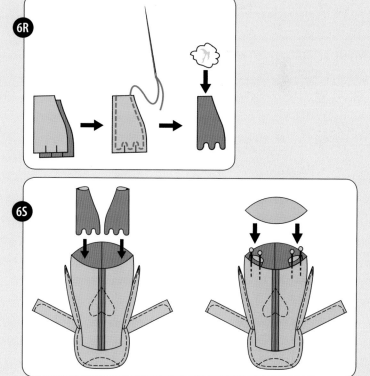

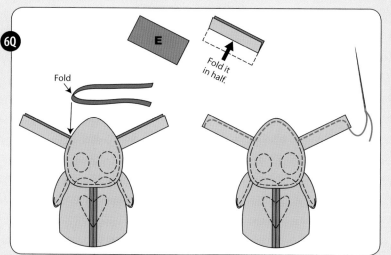

Maureen McDoover

Maureen McDoover is a retired world traveler with yarns and anecdotes for anyone who will listen. She's done it all: from pole vaulting over live volcanoes to swimming with sea monsters to flinging herself from cliffs into the ocean. As interesting as she may be, most customers of the Leftover Lounge run and hide anytime Maureen utters, "This reminds me of the time I ..."

{ *Sturdy trousers are omnipresent in closets, but they aren't always omni-stylish! That's why we're going to hack a corduroy pair to bits and reconfigure them into something nicer.* }

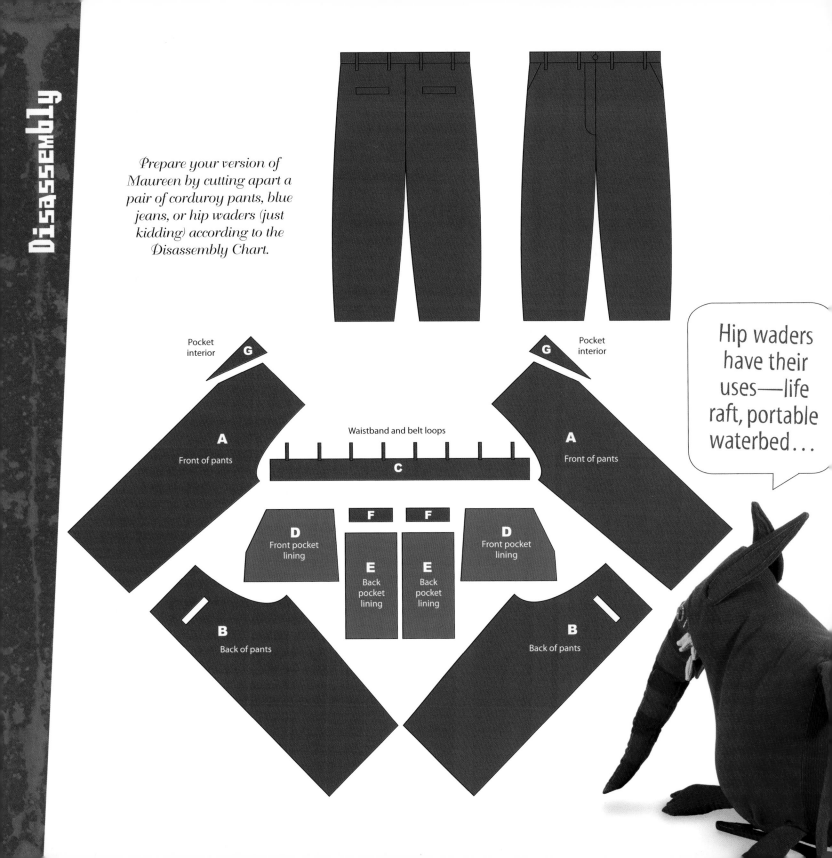

Prepare your version of Maureen by cutting apart a pair of corduroy pants, blue jeans, or hip waders (just kidding) according to the Disassembly Chart.

Pocket interior

G

A
Front of pants

Waistband and belt loops

C

G

Pocket interior

A
Front of pants

D
Front pocket lining

F

F

D
Front pocket lining

E
Back pocket lining

E
Back pocket lining

B
Back of pants

B
Back of pants

Hip waders have their uses—life raft, portable waterbed…

1. Use parts B—the back halves of the pants legs—to draw and cut Maureen's body. Use the pants' butt curve to help you visualize the contour of an animal's back leading up to its head. Draw a line for Maureen's face, neck, and chest as shown. Cut through both parts B along the line you drew. You now have the right and left sides of Maureen's body (see figure 7A).

2. Use the big remnant of part B to cut the pieces for Maureen's long nose. Refer to the line you cut for her face. Since that's already the right size for the width of her nose, fold that bit down horizontally and cut out the shape it makes. You should have a long trapezoidal form. Unfold it and lay it flat. Cut it into six or eight evenly thick strips. Bear in mind the length of the pants you're using. You can make Maureen's nose as long as you want. Turn over every other nose strip so they lay right side up and wrong side up alternately (see figure 7B).

3. Use the other big remnant from the other part B to cut the pieces for Maureen's feet. Start by folding the piece in half horizontally. Trim the piece to make an even rectangle. Cut the rectangle into four equal parts. Don't cut the folded edges. You'll need those intact (see figure 7C).

4. We'll use one of the parts A to make Maureen's chest. Fold part A in half vertically. Cut a long, curved wedge from the folded edge of part A down to its base. There is no need to measure precisely, but make the chest wedge a good 3 to 4 inches (7.6 to 10 cm) longer than the chest curve on Maureen's body. Unfold the wedge and set it aside (see figure 7D).

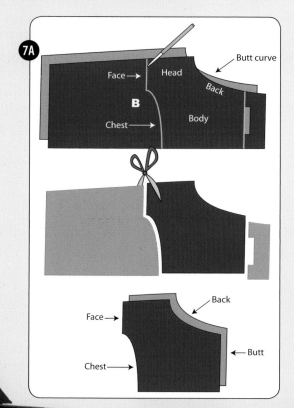

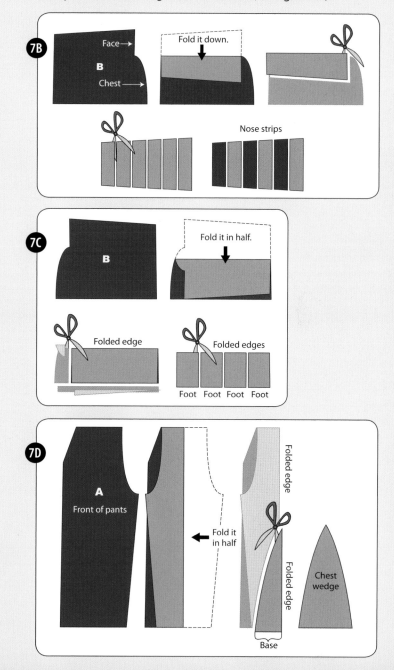

5. Continue using the same part A to cut Maureen's butt. Trim the part to create a new, flat base. For this piece, a measurement is required. Find one of the pieces you cut for Maureen's body and measure the length of her butt. Use your fashion ruler to draw an arc of the same length of Maureen's butt from the folded edge of part A to its new base. Cut along that line and unfold the shape (see figure 7E).

6. By now you should have a few long, angular scrap pieces left over from part A or some other part. Find or cut one that's at least 3 inches (7.6 cm) wide and trim it into a long, symmetrical isosceles triangle. This will be Maureen's tail (see figure 7F).

7. To cut the parts for Maureen's ears, grab a piece of pocket lining, such as part D, and lay it atop the part A that you haven't cut into yet. Draw two long, pointed ovals or whatever ear shapes you prefer. Cut the shapes out from both layers (see figure 7G).

8. Use the rest of part A to cut the shape for Maureen's body. The perimeter of this oval will be the sum of the bases of the butt wedge, the chest wedge, and both sides of Maureen's body. Refer to the Creature Feature Bottoms instructions on page 28 to use those measurements in the creation of Maureen's bottom (see figure 7H).

9. Cut out appliqués for Maureen's chest and eyes from another piece of pocket lining, such as part E (see figure 7I).

Have a look at figure 7J to see all the parts you should have cut by now. If you're short a part, remedy the situation.

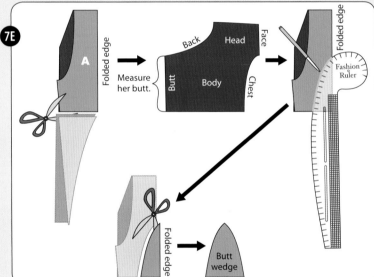

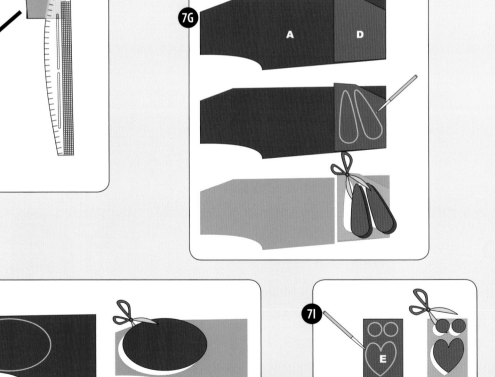

Stitching

10. Align the parts you cut for Maureen's body with right sides facing. Stitch the edge at the top of the head. Set the body aside (see figure 7K).

11. Create Maureen's nose next by sewing the alternating strips together as if you were making a Mentacle ear. Instructions for that can be found on page 26 (see figure 7L).

12. To attach Maureen's nose to her face, lay the nose right side up with its base at the top. Then lay the two body halves, which you've joined at the top of the head, atop the nose. Align the edge of Maureen's face with the base of her nose. Stitch the parts together there leaving ⅜ inch (.95 cm) of seam allowance. Now appliqué Maureen's eye patches onto her face where you think they ought to go. Find the appliqué instructions on page 33. Do any decorative top-stitching you desire at this time as well (see figures 7M and 7N).

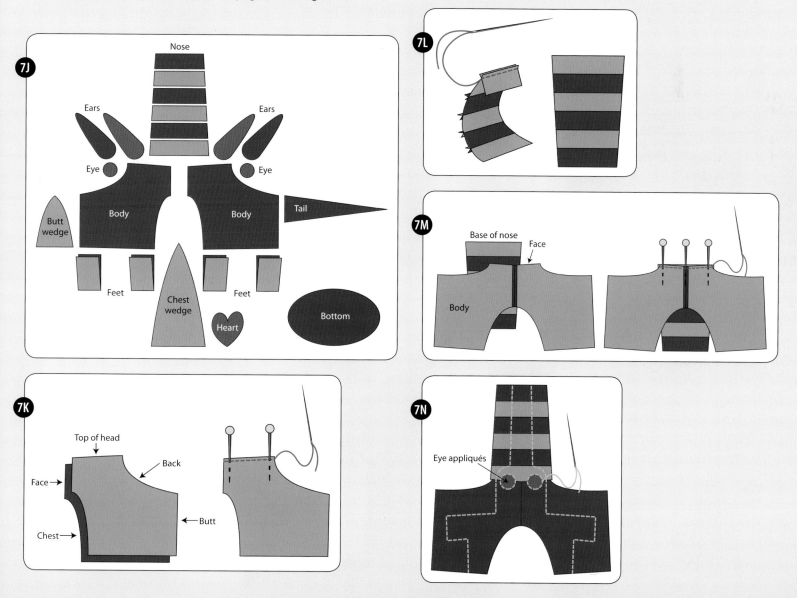

7J Nose, Ears, Ears, Eye, Eye, Body, Body, Tail, Butt wedge, Feet, Feet, Chest wedge, Heart, Bottom

7L

7M Base of nose, Face, Body

7K Top of head, Back, Face, Butt, Chest

7N Eye appliqués

13. Use the Bubble Method, found on page 32, to attach Maureen's ears (see figure 7O).

14. Once the ears are completed, arrange the body wrong side out and stitch together the edges of Maureen's back. Take care to fold the ears out of the way so you don't accidentally stitch them into that seam (see figure 7P).

15. Now, appliqué the heart (or whatever shape you've cut) to Maureen's chest wedge. Add any top-stitching you might want at this time (see figure 7Q).

16. Make Maureen some teeth, following the instructions on page 27. With the body and nose wrong side out, pin the teeth along the lower edge of Maureen's face and nose.

Refer to the Gusseted Palm arm method on page 18 to help you understand how to attach Maureen's chest wedge to her body. It's kind of similar. Align the remaining nose edges that extend beyond the tip of the chest wedge and sew them together (see figure 7R).

17. To make Maureen's tail, fold the piece you cut for the tail in half vertically with right sides touching. Stitch the open edges together leaving ³⁄₈-inch (.95 cm) seam allowance. Trim

70 — Bottom layers of the ears

7P

7Q — Chest wedge — Heart

7R — Lower edge of nose — Front edge of body — Base of chest — Wrong side out — Right side out

I still have all my own teeth.

7S — Tail — Fold it in half

the very tip of the seam allowance. Turn the tail right side out and stuff it. Leave half an inch of unstuffed space at the tail's open end (see figure 7S).

18. With the body wrong side out, align the open end of Maureen's tail with the seam at her butt and pin it into place. Align the side edges of the wedge to the edges at the back of her body and stitch it into place. The tail will be sandwiched within this seam (see figure 7T).

19. To make Maureen's feet, follow the Freefinger Arm instructions found on page 20. Stuff the feet, and leave ½ inch (1.3 cm) of space unstuffed at the open end of each foot (see figure 7U).

20. Turn Maureen wrong side out. Insert the feet, toe first, into her body and pin them where you want them to go. Attach Maureen's bottom using the Creature Feature Bottoms instructions on page 28. Leave 3 to 4 inches (7.6 to 10 cm) of this seam unstitched so you can turn and stuff Maureen (see figure 7V).

Turn Maureen right side out. Stuff her and add buttons for eyes wherever you want them to go. Maureen's nose is a perfect candidate for beanbag fill. Find tips for how to use that on page 17.

Try a pair of capri pants or sweat pants to make different versions of Maureen. Better yet, find a pair of tweedy wool trousers to give Maureen a kindly school-marmish appearance. Get inventive and enjoy the variations.

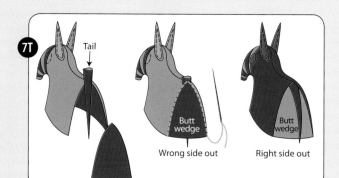

7T

Tail

Butt wedge

Wrong side out

Butt wedge

Right side out

7U

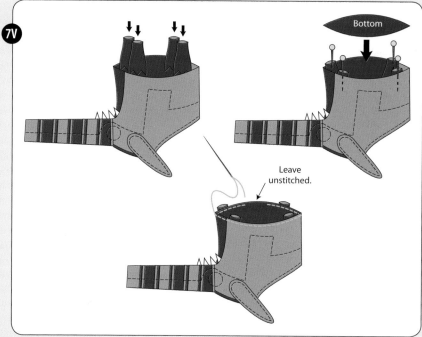

7V

Bottom

Leave unstitched.

The Mighty Glapthod

The Mighty Glapthod is a security guard. He works second shift guarding a mini-mall—his giant hands are an intimidating deterrent to criminals. However, the thingies protruding from his shoulders serve no discernible purpose at all. At the end of a shift, Glapthod heads to the Leftover Lounge to have a coffee with his best pal, Lurwin Obsgarde, before returning to his trailer to watch a game of some sort. Such is Glapthod's routine: still he prays each day for a menace to thwart so he'll have something heroic to boast about.

{ *I imagine that the owner of this acid green suit wanted to make a statement in her office environment. Hoping to be noticed for a promotion, her suit was a splash of color among the rows and rows of data she entered.* }

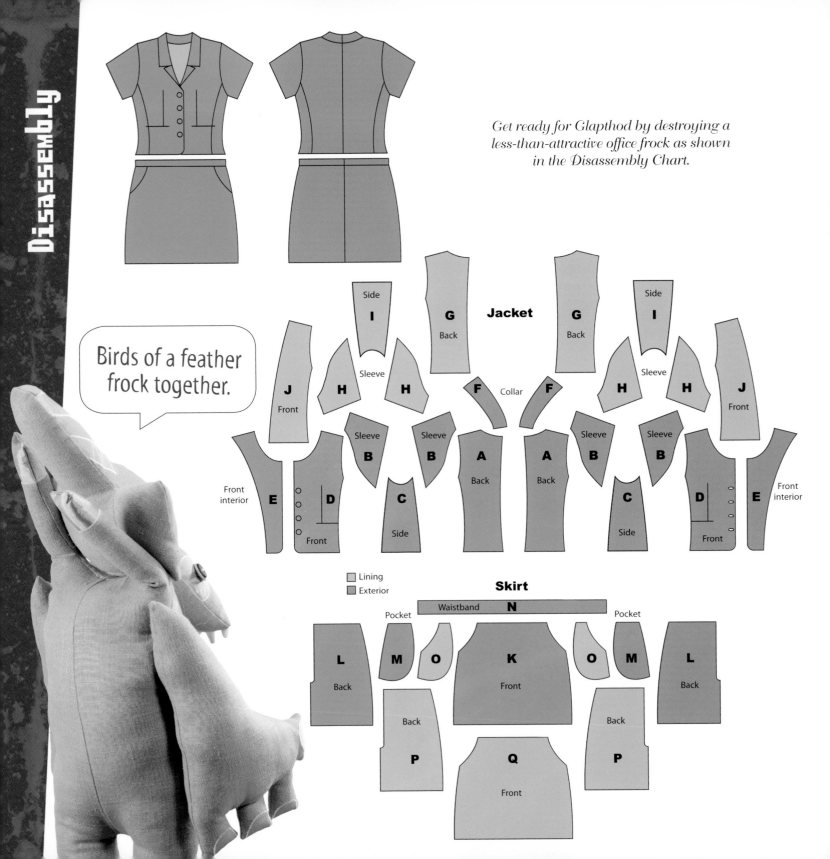

Get ready for Glapthod by destroying a less-than-attractive office frock as shown in the Disassembly Chart.

Birds of a feather frock together.

Jacket

Side
I

G
Back

G
Back

Side
I

J
Front

H

Sleeve

H

G
Back

Sleeve

F Collar F

Sleeve

H

H

J
Front

Sleeve

Sleeve

B

B

A
Back

A
Back

B

Sleeve

B

Front
interior

E

D

Front

C
Side

Back

Back

C
Side

D
Front

E

Front
interior

☐ Lining
☐ Exterior

Skirt

Waistband N

Pocket

Pocket

L
Back

M

O

K
Front

O

M

L
Back

P
Back

Q
Front

P
Back

1. I used the back panels of the skirt to create identical rectangles for Glapthod's body. Each rectangle is a side of Glapthod's body as opposed to front and back. To create the shapes for Glapthod's shoulder smokestacks, fold the body panels in half vertically, and trim a curved wedge from the corner of their open edge (see figure 8A).

2. The sleeves from the jacket yielded some incredible shapes that I used for Glapthod's big, burly arms. What you'll need are big, blocky triangles that are about half the length of Glapthod's body and as wide as you want them to be. Align two of them together with wrong sides facing. Trim the top corner to round it off a little, then cut slits into the bottom edge for fingers. Remove a square of fabric at the sleeve's bottom corner to create a "thumb" (see figure 8B).

3. To make Glapthod's head, create two long, trapezoidal shapes. I used the suit jacket's exterior side panels. Align the shapes with wrong sides facing. Round off the top, narrow edge of the shape. And there you have it (see figure 8C).

4. Use two long, rectangular forms to make Glapthod's ears. I used the two haves of the suit's collar just as they were, despite their slight curve. Perhaps the collar from your suit is similar. If not, cut vertical forms of your liking. Don't worry about how to sew them on just yet (see figure 8D).

5. We'll be making round foot pads for Glapthod's feet. Refer to the Creature Feature Bottoms instructions on page 28 to see how to do this. When you know the size you need your foot pads to be, cut them from any part of the suit that can accommodate them (see figure 8E).

6. Next you'll need to cut all of Glapthod's many appliqués from a piece of the suit's lining. You'll need six toenails that suit the size of Glapthod's feet. You'll need eight bulky fingernails that fit his stubby fingers. Cut two horizontal toppers for his shoulder-mounted smokestacks. Cut two eye patches of any size you prefer. Cut interesting shapes to adorn his forehead and face. Finally, cut a big shape to cover most of the front of Glapthod's body. On the other hand, you may pay no heed to these suggestions (see figure 8F).

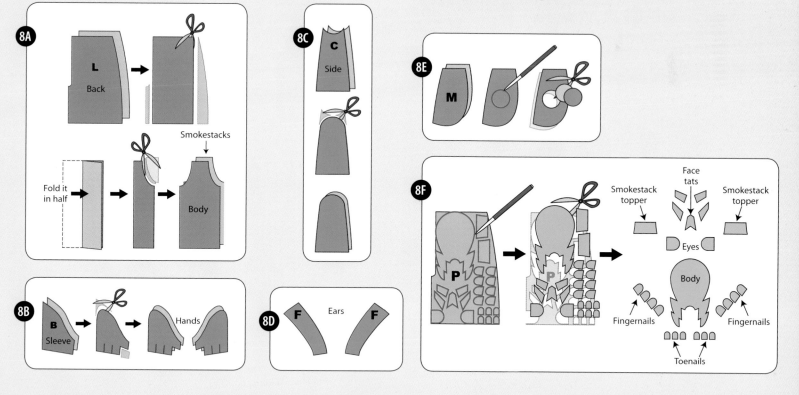

7. Cut parts for Glapthod's teeth from any tooth-colored fabric you have. See figure 8G or visit page 27 for instructions on how to make teeth.

Have a look at figure 8H to inventory all the necessary parts for Glapthod. Got them?

Stitching

8. Start assembling Glapthod by aligning his body panels together with right sides touching. Stitch down one side edge, but don't stitch the smokestacks yet. Open the body and lay it flat. Press the seam (see figure 8I).

9. Next, we'll take care of all of Glapthod's appliqué at once. Place all parts where you've designed them to go, and find instructions for adding appliqué on page 33 (see figure 8J).

10. Now, let's attach Glapthod's head and both arms using the Bubble Method on page 32. Attach the back of Glapthod's head to the front of his body first. In these diagrams, the head and arms overlap. Take care to fold the body parts away from other seams as you stitch them. If you don't, you'll regret it (see figure 8K).

11. Push the back of Glapthod's head through to the wrong side of his body. Align the front of his face with the back of his head, with right sides touching, and stitch the edges at the upper curve of his head. Do not stitch the rest of his head shut yet. Grab the parts you cut for Glapthod's ears. Fold them in half horizontally with the wrong sides touching. Attach them to Glapthod's head using the Arc Method found on page 30. Make Glapthod's teeth, and insert them, point first, into his face. Find instructions for making teeth on page 27. When the ears are attached, stitch them shut on the sides and bottoms. Stitch shut the rest of Glapthod's face, fastening the teeth into place (see figures 8L, 8M, and 8N).

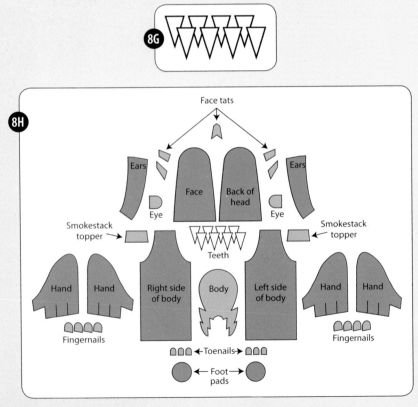

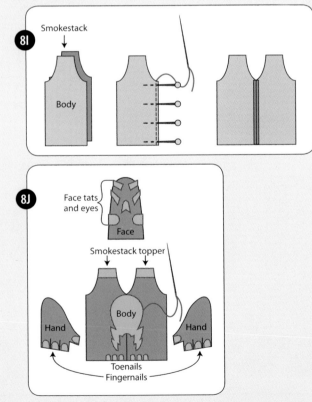

12. Push Glapthod's completed head back through the hole to the right side of his body. Use the Bubble Method, found on page 32, to stitch the right sides of his hands to their corresponding wrong sides (see figure 8O).

13. Fold Glapthod's body panels together with right sides touching, concealing his head within. Match the side edges and stitch them together leaving ³⁄₈-inch (.95 cm) seam allowance. Make sure you don't get Glapthod's head stuck in the seam (see figure 8P).

14. Stuff Glapthod's head deep into his body, out of the way of the smokestacks' edges. Stitch the smokestacks closed at their tops and partially down their sides. Leave 3 or 4 inches (7.6 to 10 cm) of space unstitched between the smokestacks for turning and stuffing. Create legs for Glapthod using the Add-A-Stub method found on page 24 (see figure 8Q).

15. Attach Glapthod's foot pads using the Round Creature Bottom instructions on page 28. The suit I used wasn't stretchy so attaching foot pads was a slightly less forgiving process but it still worked (see figure 8R).

16. Turn Glapthod right side out, and stuff him through the opening between his smokestacks. Close him up using the closing stitch found on page 16.

This particular creature was an adventure. Loads of Bubble Method, I know, but now you're a pro at it. Try making Glapthod from a men's suit next or perhaps a yellow slicker to give Glapthod a cautionary look for future miscreants.

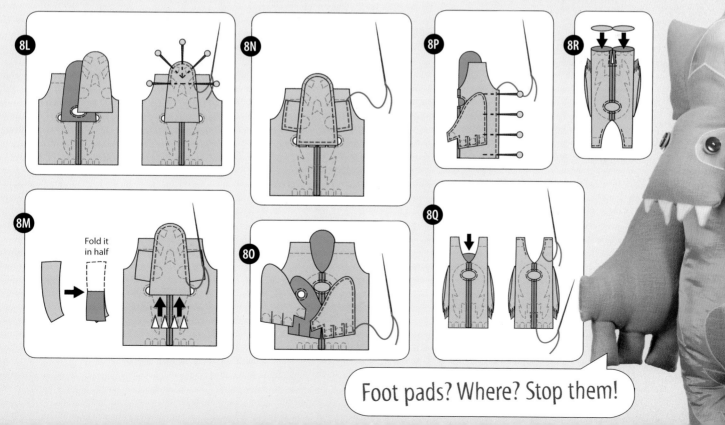

Foot pads? Where? Stop them!

Zazmyrna Hoag

Retired film star and serial spouse, Mrs. Zazmyrna Myerbag-Danvitch-Glapthire-Hoag whiles away her time with a tumbler in one hand and romance novel in the other—spreading laughter, joy, and gossip to her neighbors. After decades of acting and many marriages, Zazmyrna can finally live her three-eyed life without tethers. Daytime TV, bridge with the girls, and box after box of chocolate cordials is all Zazmyrna needs to be happy.

{ *This dress brings to mind a closet in a small, coastal cottage (or a trailer) surrounded by citrus trees and aging neighbors. The garish colors and vertigo-inducing, floral pattern will make a creature that's vivid, lively, and oh-so-sassy.* }

The dress I used yielded parts so big they didn't lend themselves to single body part shapes. Disassemble your muumuu or house dress as I've done in the Disassembly Chart or in any way that yields you great, flat panels of fabric. (I will show you how to draw templates for this creature.) Look at the cutting diagrams for inspiration or photocopy and enlarge them if you must.

D Neck wrap thing

C Sleeve

C Sleeve

A Back of the dress

B Front of the dress

B Front of the dress

A good housedress is less of a "bag" and more of a "drape."

1. On sturdy paper, draw and cut out a body shape for Zazmyrna with two stubby legs. Also draw a stout blocky head (see figure 9A).

2. Use the body template to determine the size of Zazmyrna's dress. Lay the body shape atop some paper and sketch a big arc around it—as full as you want the dress to be. Sketch the top edge of the dress about 1 inch (2.5 cm) away from the top edge of the body shape. Cut out the dress template (see figure 9B).

3. Create a second body template on sturdy paper—this one will be for Zazmyrna's back. Cut the body template horizontally where you think the middle of her butt might occur. Lay the two pieces on top another sheet of paper. Keep the cut edges parallel and separate them by 2 inches (5 cm) or so. Trace the body shapes, and stop where the space between them occurs. Draw 3/8-inch (.95 cm) lines down from the corner of the upper body, and up from the corner of the legs to accommodate a seam allowance. Then connect those little lines with a V pointing sideways. The V can go as deep into the body as you want, but 1 1/2 to 2 inches (3.3 to 5 cm) is a good ballpark. When your darts

are drawn and measured properly, cut out the back template (see figure 9C). And when you're done with all that, tape the front of the body templates back together again. Whew!

4. Grab both parts B. Trace the head template twice, and the front and back body templates once. Cut out all the parts. Reserve the leftovers from parts B for appliqués or things like that. Align both parts C with wrong sides facing. Trace the dress template and cut it out. You should have two layers for Zazmyrna's frumpy, fabulous dress (see figures 9D and 9E).

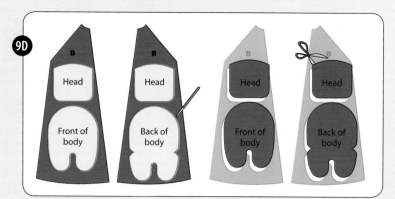

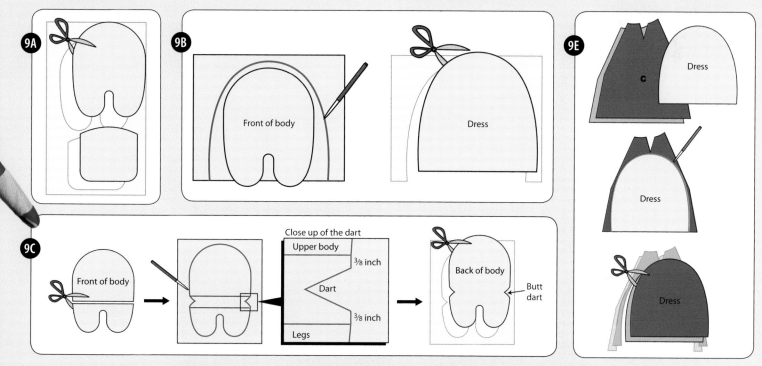

5. Fold part A—the back of the dress—in half vertically. Place the head template atop the folded fabric, with the top of the head at the folded edge. Trace the head, but don't trace the top of it. Let the lines at the sides of the head extend to the fabric's fold—this will be the inside of Zazmyrna's mouth.

Draw two identical freeform arms and two sleeves that are wider than the arms by 1 inch (2.5 cm) or more on all sides. Finally, draw a long triangle from which we'll make Zazmyrna's ears. You can make this triangle as long as you want, or as your fabric yields. Cut out all the parts you drew. You should have two layers for every shape you made, except for the mouth interior. Do not cut it. That part is its folded edge: you'll want it whole (see figures 9F and 9G).

6. Keep the ear triangles aligned and cut them into evenly thick strips. Make sure your strips are in the neighborhood of 2½ inches (6.3 cm) wide (see figure 9H).

7. From scrap fabric, cut three identical circles for Zazmyrna's eyes. Cut also a pouty, lippy shape for her mouth (see figure 9I).

8. Cut about one-third of the length of the neck-wrap thing out of the middle. We'll use the ends for Zazmyrna's neck wrap thing (see figure 9J).

Have a look at figure 9K to see all the parts we've prepared for Zazmyrna. If you've fallen short by any stretch, perform a citizen's arrest upon yourself.

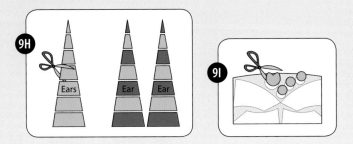

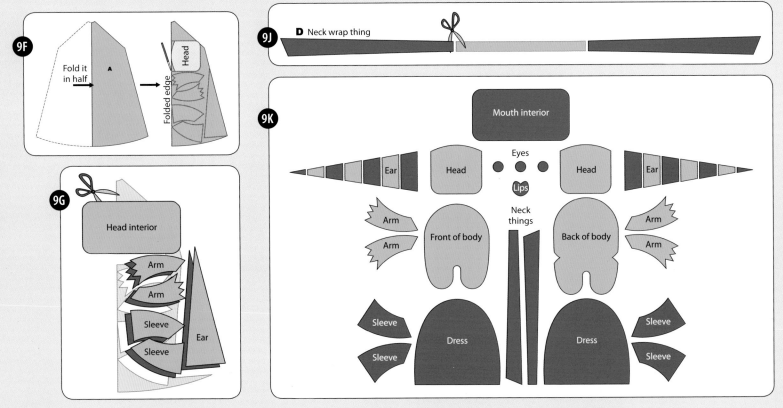

Stitching

9. Appliqué Zazmyrna's eyes and lips to the front of her face using the right side of the fabric to contrast with her face. Lay the mouth interior vertically, right side up. Lay the face atop the mouth interior, appliqué side down, and match the bottom edges of both shapes. Pin the shapes together. Draw a smile line where you see the stitches that hold the lips into place. Stitch around that line, leaving ⅜ inch (.95 cm) of seam allowance all the way around (see figure 9L).

10. Carefully cut through both the face and the mouth interior along the line you drew across Zazmyrna's lips. Notch the seam allowance at the corners of her smile. Push the face through the mouth, and lay it flat, appliqué side up atop the mouth interior. Stitch around the edge of the mouth to stabilize the seam. Fold the mouth interior downward behind the face. Match all edges at the bottom of the face, and place a few pins to hold it all together (see figure 9M).

11. Use the Bubble Method found on page 32 to attach the back of Zazmyrna's head to the front of her body. Sandwich one layer of her dress and the cut ends of her neck between her head and body where you intend for them to connect. Make sure the neck ties are stitched into place between the head and other layers. Continue following the Bubble Method to attach Zazmyrna's face the back of her head. Stitch only the top edge at this time (see figures 9N and 9O).

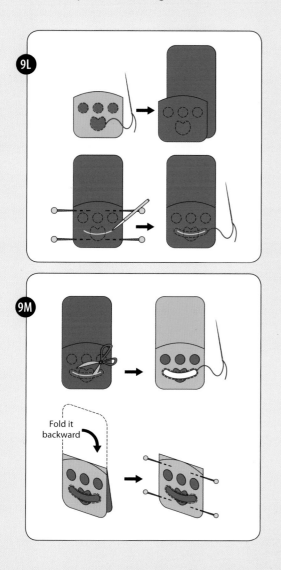

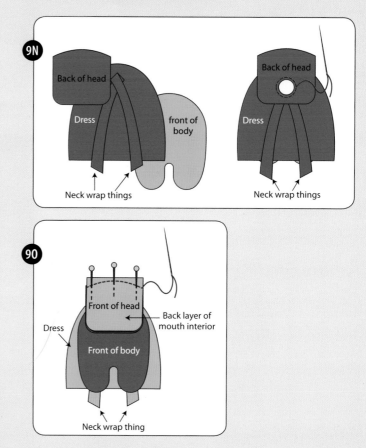

12. Follow the Mentacle Ears instructions on page 26 to create Zazmyrna's ears. Attach Zazmyrna's ears to her head using the Arc Method on page 30 (see figures 9P and 9Q).

13. Turn Zazmyrna over and position the other layer of her dress atop the first layer. Align them both with right sides facing, and stitch the shoulder edges together. Don't stitch all the way down yet (see figure 9R).

14. Align Zazmyrna's sleeve parts together with right sides touching. Stitch their top edges together. Attach Zazmyrna's sleeves to her dress using the Arc Method found on page 30. Finish stitching the sides of her dress all the way down to her feet. Make sure to notch the seam allowance at the armpits (see figures 9S and 9T).

15. Flip Zazmyrna over. Use the sleeves of her dress as a reference point and place pins in her body where the arms will attach. This step is a must if you want Zazmyrna's arms to go into her sleeves without a problem (see figure 9U).

16. Align Zazmyrna's arm parts together with the wrong sides of the fabric facing. We're using the wrong side of the fabric as Zazmyrna's skin anyway so try not to let this step confuse you. Follow the Freefinger Arm instructions on page 20 to assemble Zazmyrna's arms. Stuff the arms, leaving 1/2 inch (1.3 cm) of unstuffed space at the open end (see figure 9V). If you want to use beanbag fill in her fingers, do that before you stuff (page 17).

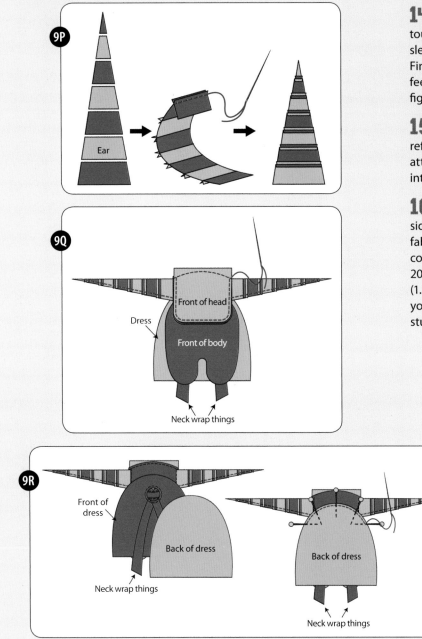

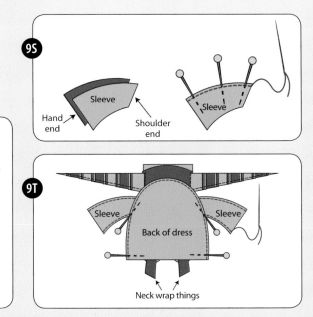

17. Stuff Zazmyrna's dress into her head through her neck hole. It's a strange thing to do, but it's necessary so you can sew the rest of Zazmyrna's body together.

Lay Zazmyrna's arms atop her body exactly below the pins you placed using the sleeves as a reference. Pin the arms into place. Fold the back of Zazmyrna's body, right side out, at the darts in her butt. Stitch the darts together.

Lay the back of Zazmyrna's body matching and pinning all the edges. Stitch around the whole shape, clamping the arms into place. Leave a good 4-inch (10 cm) space unstitched in her side for turning and stuffing (see figures 9W, 9X, and 9Y).

18. Now, with great patience and care, ease Zazmyrna's dress out of her head and through the stuffing hole in the side of her body. Once her dress is out, shimmy the rest of her head and body out through the stuffing hole as well. When that's all taken care of, you can put her dress on right and get her arms in the sleeves. Stuff her through the hole in her side. Close her up with the closing stitch found on page 16 (see figure 9Z).

Try using buttons as pupils for Zazmyrna's eyes. If you don't have a muumuu or hideous house dress, try a tatty bathrobe or a night gown. For a really freaky set of textures and effects, use a cloth shower curtain. Have fun!

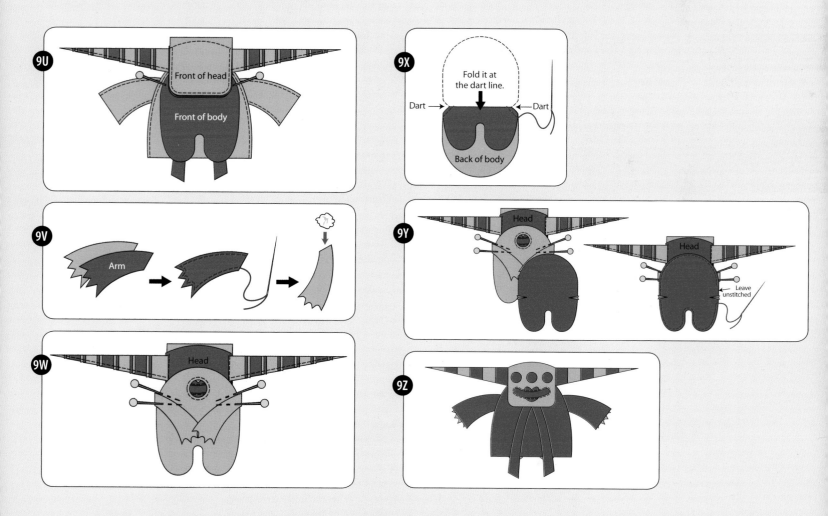

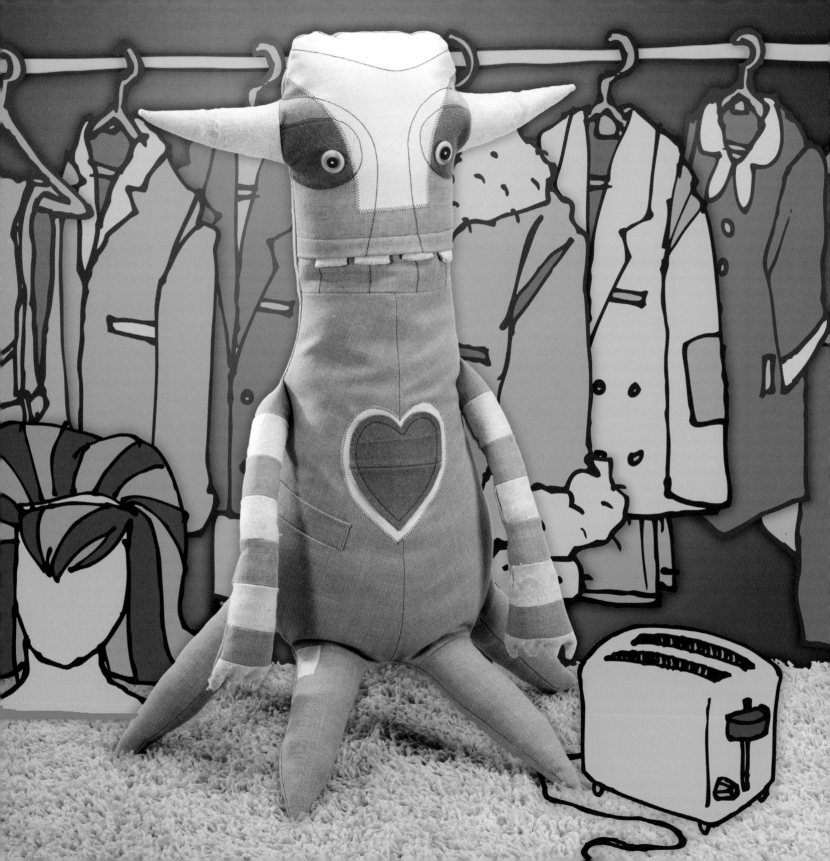

Julian Van Voon

Julian Van Voon, hospital orderly by day and domestic maven by night, is a lover of mid-century kitsch, vintage china patterns, and film noir femmes fatale. Julian loves card games, mostly for the excuse to make attractive finger sandwiches. The neighborhood housewives love him because he's more than glad to share his secrets of domestic mastery.

{ *The pastel color isn't what one normally expects in a man's blazer. I can imagine several possibilities for the life led by its wearer: television evangelist, door-to-door makeup salesman, or aging golf pro. Can't you?* }

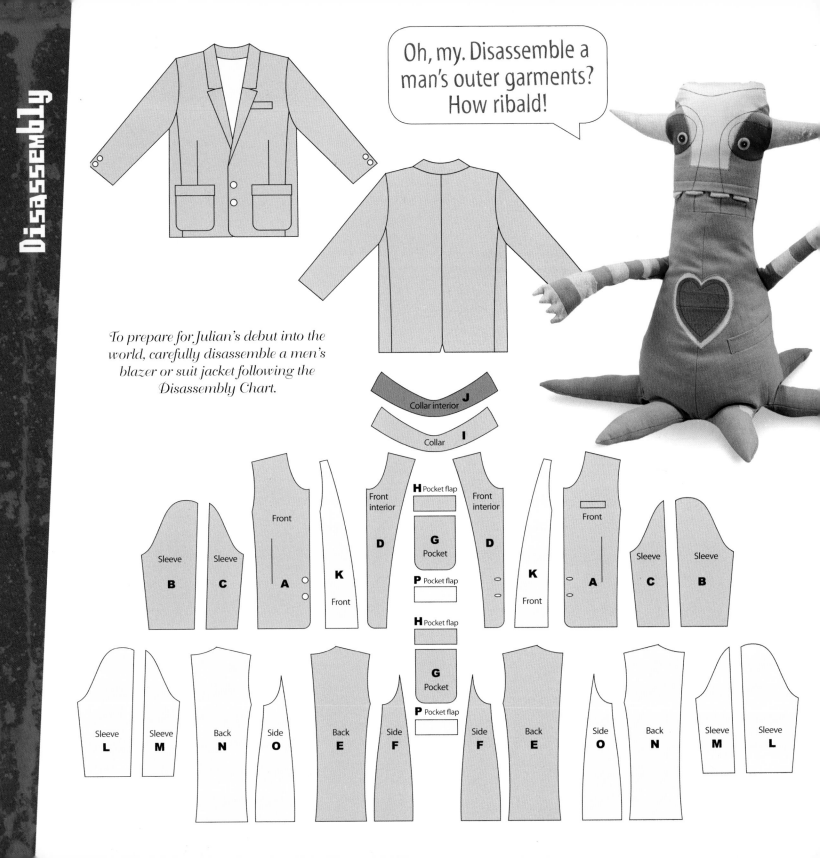

Oh, my. Disassemble a man's outer garments? How ribald!

To prepare for Julian's debut into the world, carefully disassemble a men's blazer or suit jacket following the Disassembly Chart.

Collar interior **J**

Collar **I**

Sleeve **B**

Sleeve **C**

Front **A**

K Front

Front interior **D**

H Pocket flap

G Pocket

P Pocket flap

Front interior **D**

K Front

Front **A**

Sleeve **C**

Sleeve **B**

H Pocket flap

G Pocket

P Pocket flap

Sleeve **L**

Sleeve **M**

Back **N**

Side **O**

Back **E**

Side **F**

Side **F**

Back **E**

Side **O**

Back **N**

Sleeve **M**

Sleeve **L**

1. Since I plan to use the exterior pockets (parts G) for Julian's head, I must first measure them to determine how large I should cut the parts for his body. Measure the top edge of part G, divide that measurement in half, and add ⅜ inch (.95 cm) to it. This will be half the width of Julian's neck, plus seam allowance. Write down that measurement for the next step (see figure 10A).

2. Align parts E with wrong sides touching. Align parts A with wrong sides touching. Then stack all four layers together, matching their shoulder edges. Use the measurement you took from part G (in step 1) for the top of the trapezoidal shape. Cut the shape out along the line you drew. Each shape will serve as one-quarter of Julian's body (see figure 10B).

3. Use the parts G as the front and back of the head, and one of the pocket flaps, part H, as the lower jaw. I used the other pocket flap to make Julian's teeth, since on its wrong side, it was covered with white fusible interfacing, giving it a distinct look (see figure 10C). You may use whatever you like to make teeth for Julian. Just follow the tooth-making instructions on page 27.

4. Make Julian's forehead and nose next. Trace the rounded edge of one of the parts G, which are reserved for Julian's head, onto a piece of lining material. Remove part G and draw the shape you want for Julian's nose. Cut that shape out. It will be appliquéd to the front of Julian's face (see figure 10D).

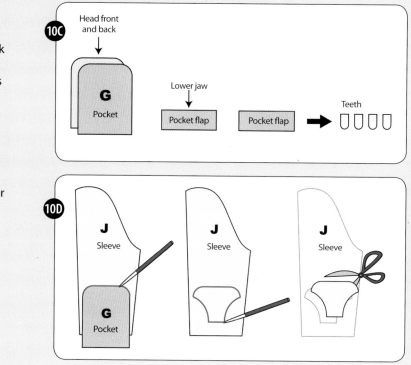

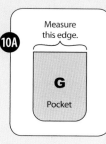

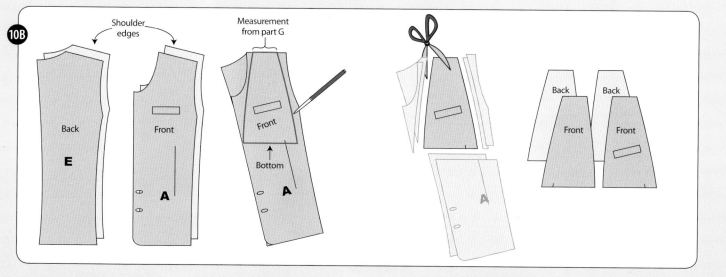

5. My jacket had a piece of thick felt sewn onto the underside of its collar. I used it to make Julian's eye patches and the heart shape for his chest. Use whatever parts your garment yields to make appliqué shapes (see figure 10E).

6. Find long, narrow pieces of jacket (like part F) to make Julian's striped arms. Align the parts with wrong sides facing, and trim the top and bottom edges flat. Cut the resulting shape into six or eight strips of the same width. Turn the strips wrong side up alternately to provide the striped look for Julian's arms. My coat was covered with permanent fusible interfacing, giving one side a distinctive chalky look. Use strips from similar fabric from other projects it you want to make even more colorful arms. I wouldn't use a lining material: it's just too thin for sewing and stuffing (see figure 10F).

7. Cut remnants of part E into triangular palms for Julian's arms. For his horns, cut a big oval, a little wider than Julian's head and perhaps half as tall. Cut that shape into vertical halves (see figure 10G).

8. Use the Creature Feature Bottom instructions on page 28 to create a bottom for Julian (see figure 10H).

9. To make Julian's six stubby tentacles, you'll need to cut 12 identical shapes that are essentially triangles with curved sides. Cut these shapes from whatever fabric you have left. You probably won't be able to cut all of the leg parts from one single piece of the coat (see figure 10I).

Take a look at figure 10J to see the vast inventory of parts we need for making Julian. If you lack anything shown, seek therapy, then do what you must to get up to speed.

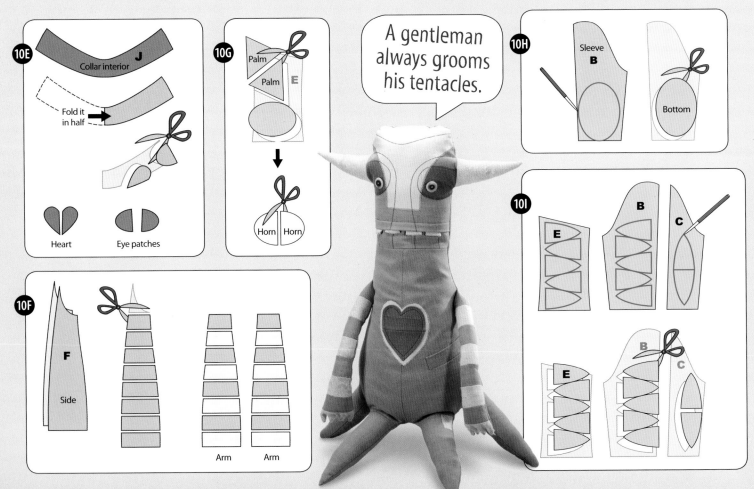

Stitching

10.   Appliqué the eye patches to Julian's face where you think they ought to go. Overlay the part you cut for his nose and align it with the top of his head. Appliqué that into place. Then add any top-stitching you may want (see figure 10K).

11.   Lay the face right side up. Align the open edges of the teeth with the bottom edge of the face. Lay part H atop the teeth, and align its bottom edge with the bottom edge of the face. Stitch the whole stack together leaving ⅜-inch (.95 cm) seam allowance, fastening the teeth into place (see figure 10L).

12.   Align the parts you cut for the front of Julian's body together with right sides touching. Stitch them together along the chest edge leaving ⅜-inch (.95 cm) seam allowance. Lay

the attached parts flat and press the seam. Repeat these steps for the back of Julian's body, but leave about 4 inches (10 cm) of the seam unstitched in the center of his back for turning and stuffing (see figure 10M).

13.   Now's the time to attach any appliqué you desire to the front of Julian's body (see figure 10N). Find instructions for appliqué on page 33.

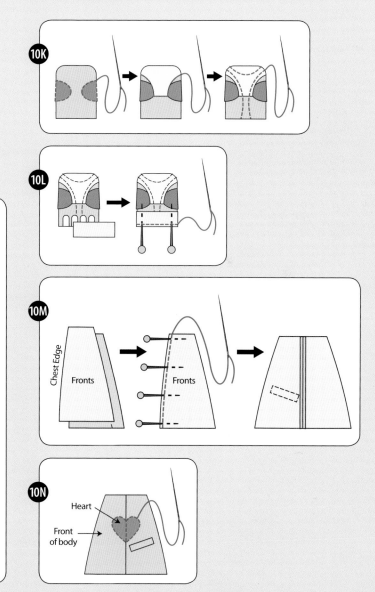

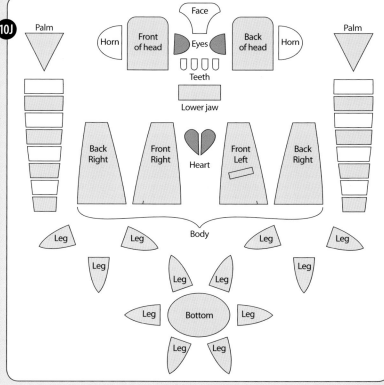

14. Lay Julian's face atop the front side of his body with right sides facing. Match the top edge of the body with the bottom edge of the face, and stitch along those edges leaving ⅜-inch (.95 cm) seam allowance. Do the same with the back of Julian's head and the back of his body. Lay the attached heads and bodies flat and press the seams. Top-stitch Julian's back (see figures 10O and 10P).

15. Julian's lower jaw adds length to his face. To make the face match the size of the back of his head, fold a bit of it over into a flap that partially conceals the teeth. This will give the illusion of an upper lip. Once that's done, fasten the flap into place by straight stitching about ½ inch (1.3 cm) up from its folded edge (see figure 10Q).

16. Lay the back of Julian's body atop the front. Match all the edges together, and stitch around the crown of his head leaving ⅜-inch (.95 cm) seam allowance (see figure 10R).

17. Pick up the half-ovals you cut for Julian's horns and fold them in half, matching the curved edges, with right sides facing. Attach them to Julian's head using the Arc Method found on page 30. Once that's done, stitch the rest of Julian's head closed, leaving ⅜-inch (.95 cm) seam allowance, and continue stitching down the outside edges of his body about one-quarter to one-third of the way, or however far down you want his arms to attach (see figure 10S).

18. Assemble Julian's arms by sewing the alternating strips together as if you were making a Mentacle ear (page 26). Once the arms are assembled, combine them with the parts you cut for the palms to make Gusseted Palm arms (page 18).

Stuff the arms and leave ½ inch (1.2 cm) of unstuffed space at their open end. Insert Julian's arms into his body. Make sure the palm side of his arms are touching the front side of his body. Attach the arms using the Tuck and Sew Method found on page 30 (see figures 10T, 10U, and 10V).

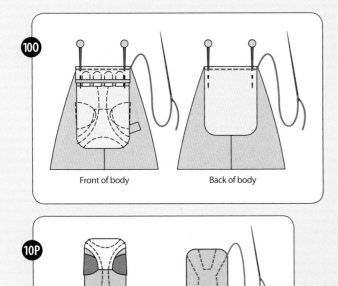

10O — Front of body / Back of body

10P — Front of body / Back of body

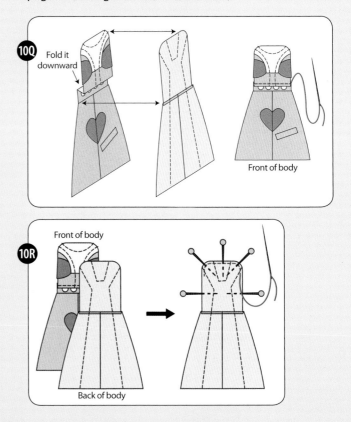

10Q — Fold it downward / Front of body

10R — Front of body / Back of body

19. Turn Julian right side out. Pin six of his leg flaps, evenly spaced, around his body with right sides touching. Stitch the legs onto Julian's body leaving ⅜-inch (.95 cm) seam allowance. Similarly, evenly space the remaining leg flaps, with right sides touching around the perimeter of Julian's bottom. Stitch them into place leaving ⅜-inch (.95 cm) seam allowance (see figure 10W).

20. Now that you've got the legs evenly spaced on Julian's body and bottom, turn the body wrong side out again. Align the bottom set of legs with the legs on the body. Pin all the corners and tips, which might take you a good year and a half. Stitch around the matched edges leaving ⅜-inch (.95 cm) seam allowance. Remember to notch and trim the points and corners of this whole business. And that's it. You're done assembling Julian!!

21. Turn him right side out very carefully and with great patience through the opening you left in his back. It's best to get his arms out first then shimmy the rest out very gently. Get a masseuse to help you. Once that's done, stuff Julian. Use the closing stitch from page 16 to sew the hole shut.

Give Julian a bit of life by sewing buttons onto his eye patches.

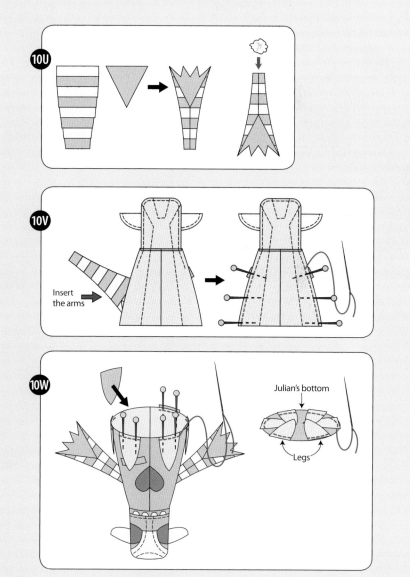

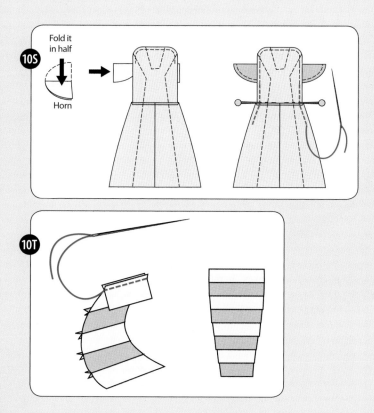

Blarty Dween

Blarty Dween is an over-anxious 'tween who spends his free time rappelling, cliff diving, swimming with sharks, and white water rafting. Alas, these (and other) dangerous adventures have not made him braver. So, before each new challenge, he soothes his fears sipping warm milk at the Leftover Lounge, where his long-time pal Camilla Grace reminds him to take his pills.

{ *Ah, cargo pants—more pockets and flaps than anyone needs, plus zippy legs that you can remove! This piece of clothing was an interesting design challenge for this book, but I think you're going to like this project.* }

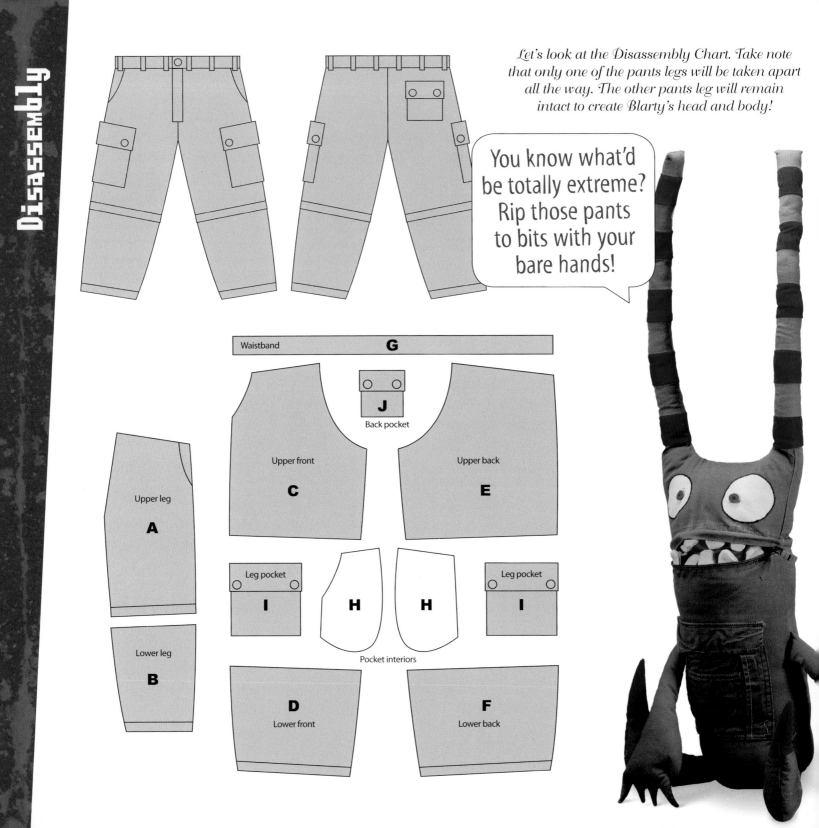

Disassembly

Let's look at the Disassembly Chart. Take note that only one of the pants legs will be taken apart all the way. The other pants leg will remain intact to create Blarty's head and body!

You know what'd be totally extreme? Rip those pants to bits with your bare hands!

Waistband **G**

J
Back pocket

Upper front
C

Upper back
E

Upper leg
A

Leg pocket
I

H

H

Leg pocket
I

Pocket interiors

Lower leg
B

Lower front
D

Lower back
F

1. Trim the cuff of the pants leg you didn't disassemble parallel with the zipper. Cut the upper part of the pants leg into a segment as large as you want Blarty's head to be.

2. Turn Blarty's body (the uncut pants leg) wrong side out. Trim off the side seams along the sides. Stop a few inches below the zipper 'cause you really don't want that coming apart. It'll be a pain to reassemble so leave it alone. You'll need this seam open for attaching Blarty's arms and cargo pocket (see figures 11A and 11B).

3. Cut the parts for Blarty's ears from a big piece of pants material. Part F is perfect for this. Align it with fabric of similar substance and contrasting color (I used leftovers from making Maureen). Trim both pieces into two equal rectangles at least 5 inches (12.7 cm) wide. Cut the rectangles horizontally into as many 2½-inch (6.3 cm) strips as your rectangles will yield (see figure 11C).

4. To cut the parts for Blarty's arms, use another piece of flat pants material. Part D will do. Fold it in half vertically. Cut two tall, trapezoidal shapes from the fabric.

Next, follow the Gusseted Palm arm instructions on page 18, and cut two triangular palms from different fabric (see figure 11D).

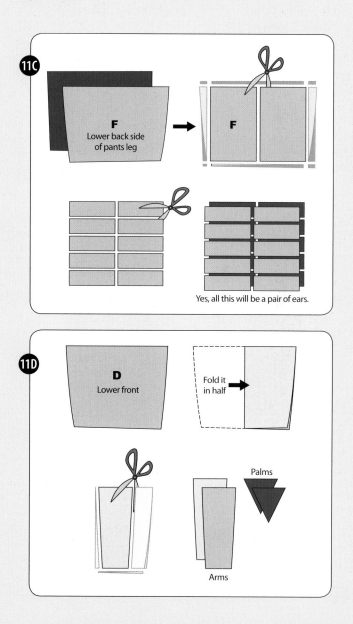

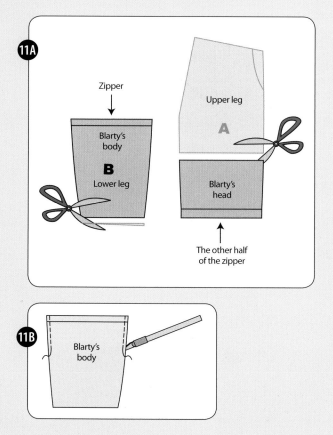

5. Follow the instructions for the Dangly Leg with a Different Colored Toe and No Sole on page 22 to make Blarty's feet. I trimmed part E into a rectangle, which provided the base part for the legs I made for Blarty. The toes were cut from more leftover material from making Maureen (see figure 11E).

6. Use a remnant or an unused piece of pants fabric for Blarty's round bottom. Reread the instructions on page 28 if you don't remember how to make one.

7. Use the pocket lining to cut big round eyes for Blarty and to make his teeth (see figure 11F). Make them using the instructions on page 27.

8. Measure the width of the zippered edge of Blarty's body. Use the same method you used for Blarty's bottom to calculate the size of two identical ovals for the lower and upper interiors of his mouth.

Make a big tongue from different fabric, following the tongue instructions on page 27. Cut a patch of dark fabric, from another source, that will give the illusion of a uvula and throat for Blarty's mouth (see figure 11G).

Review figure 11H to see all the parts we should have by now to put together a Blarty. If you are missing anything, heat up a tablespoon of I-know-you-didn't and sauté yourself in shame.

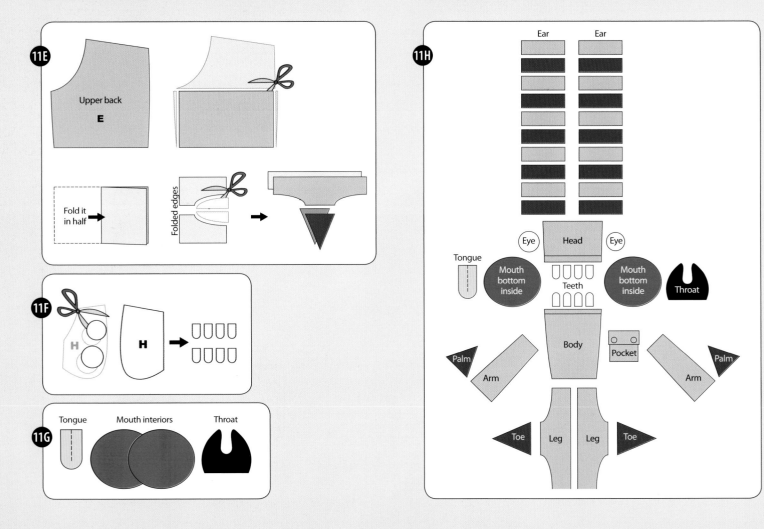

Stitching

9. Follow the Dangly Leg with a Different Colored Toe and No Sole instructions on page 22 to construct Blarty's feet.

Use the Gusseted Palm instructions on page 18 to create Blarty's arms. Stuff them, and leave ½ inch (1.3 cm) of unstuffed space at the open end (see figures 11I and 11J).

10. Stitch the pants pocket to Blarty's body wherever you think it should go. Once the pocket is attached, turn the body wrong side out. Insert the arms between the two layers and attach them using the Tuck and Sew Method found on page 30 (see figures 11K and 11L).

11. To attach the mouth correctly, you'll need to do a little prep work. Look at the zipper assembly on the inside of the pants leg. Stitched in between the zipper and the pants, most cargo pants feature a flap which serves to hide the zipper when the pants are worn. Typically, the pants, the flap, and the zipper are held together with a standard attaching seam (shown in red), and then the raw edges of all three items are stitched to the inside of the pants leg with a stabilizing seam (shown in blue). Use your seam ripper or craft knife to remove just the stabilizing seam. Don't remove the seam holding the zipper and flap to the pants. When the seam is removed, fold the assembly upward so that the flap's folded edge is pointing down, and the raw edges of all the layers are pointing up. Once this is done you can proceed with installing Blarty's mouth, tongue, and teeth (see figure 11M).

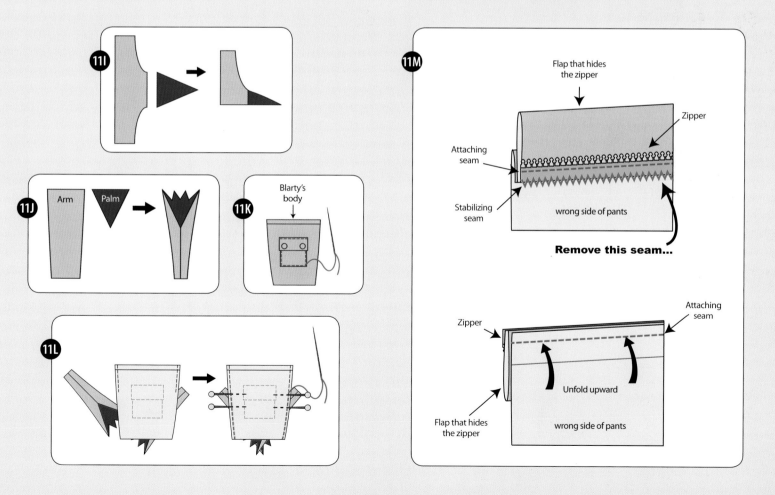

12. Turn Blarty's body wrong side out. Align the open edges of his teeth to the front of Blarty's body at the raw edge of the pants and zipper. Align the open edge of his tongue to the back of his body in the same manner you did the teeth. Pin all teeth and tongues into place. Follow the Creature Feature Bottoms instructions on page 28 to attach the interior of the mouth (see figure 11N).

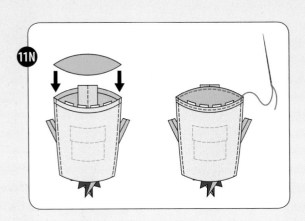

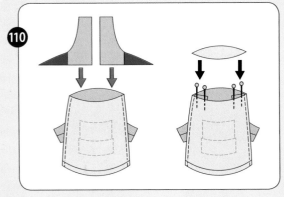

13. Insert Blarty's legs into the bottom of his body. Pin their open edges to the corners of the front of his body. Attach the bottom of his body using the Creature Feature Bottoms instructions found on page 28. Leave 4 inches (10 cm) of the bottom unstitched in the back for turning and stuffing (see figure 11O).

At this point, you should have a partially decapitated but otherwise complete creature. You'll stuff and close the body independently of the head (see figure 11P).

14. Appliqué Blarty's eyes onto his face. Appliqué Blarty's throat to the remaining mouth interior. Trim any parts that over hang the edge of the oval as needed (see figures 11Q and 11R).

15. Assemble Blarty's ears as you would a Mentacle Ear (page 26). Then, attach the ears to Blarty's head using the Add-A-Stub leg method on page 24. Leave the space between the ears unstitched for turning and stuffing (see figures 11S and 11T).

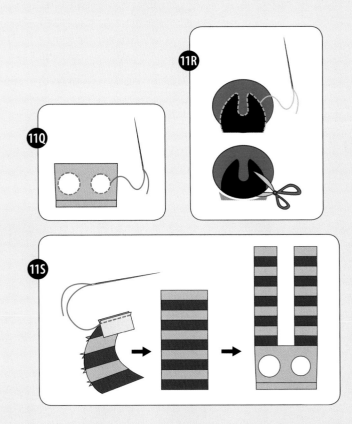

16. Follow the Creature Feature Bottoms instructions on page 28 to attach the mouth interior (see figure 11U).

17. Turn Blarty's head right side out. Stuff it through the hole between his ears. Make sure you stuff the ears first before filling out his head. Close the stuffing hole with a closing stitch (see figure 11V).

18. Zip Blarty's head to his body. Close his mouth all the way, or unzip it just a tad. It's entirely up to you. Shock a friend by removing Blarty's entire head and throwing it at him. Scream a bit also for the right effect.

> Anybody got antacid? This stuff is terrifying!

You don't need to stick with zippy-legged cargo pants to make a decent Blarty Dween. If you know how to install zippers, you can use other kinds of pants. Use a pair of camouflage pants to make a stealth Blarty or a pair of carpenter's pants for work-a-day Blarty.

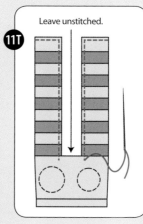

Leave unstitched.

11T

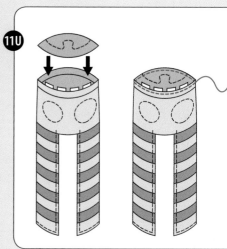

11U

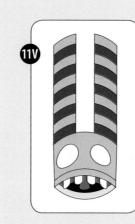

11V

BooFaye Bovelle Bernadella

BooFaye Bovelle Bernadella: the Belle of the Ball, Queen Bee, and Top of the Social Food Chain. She plans every wedding in town, dresses all the debutantes, and has her fingers in every tea party, antique shoppe, bake sale, and bachelor auction in town. She scorns the famous TV shows of domestic divas, because whatever they just did she's done for years—from whom do you think they learned it??

{ *This classic jacket design is in just about every woman's closet—though perhaps not in these colors or with the pearly trim. Chances are the person who wore this jacket was a perfect southern lady whose potato salad is the creamiest and who seems to know (and will tell you) your business before you even know it.* }

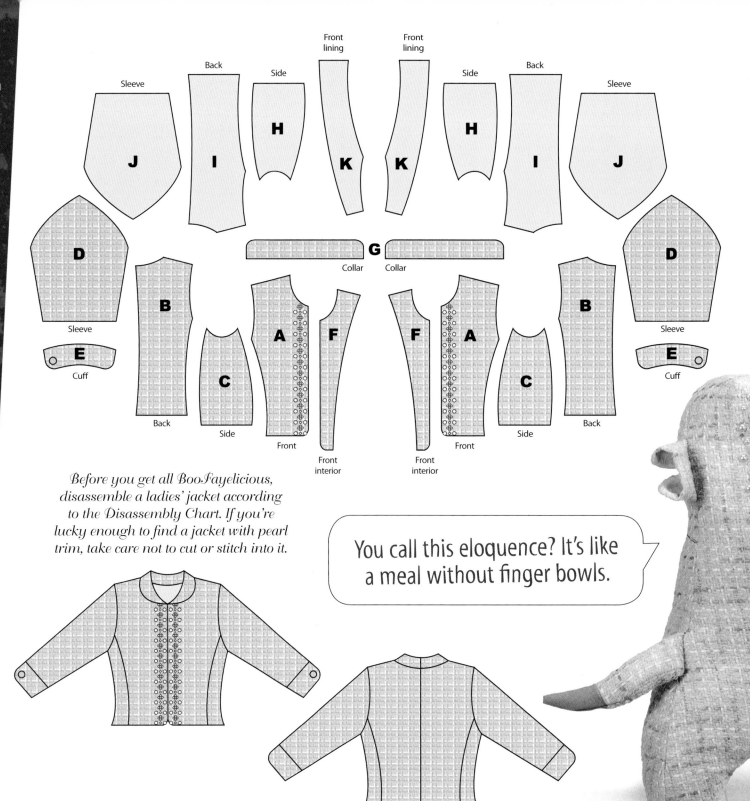

Sleeve
Back
Side
Front lining
Front lining
Side
Back
Sleeve

J I H K K H I J

D
G
Collar Collar
D
Sleeve
Sleeve

B B

E E
Cuff Cuff

A F F A
Back Side Back
C C
Side
Front Front
Front interior Front interior

Before you get all BooFayelicious, disassemble a ladies' jacket according to the Disassembly Chart. If you're lucky enough to find a jacket with pearl trim, take care not to cut or stitch into it.

You call this eloquence? It's like a meal without finger bowls.

1. Align both parts A and B wrong sides together with the shoulder edges pointing down. Stack both all the parts aligning their sleeve curves and shoulder edges. Imagine the sleeve curve and shoulder edge as BooFaye's leg and foot. Draw the shape you want BooFaye's body to be and trim along the line you drew.

I used the back of the jacket (parts B) for the front of the body, if you can believe that. To give the face some roundness, trim the

corner opposite the side edge of BooFaye's body. You should now have all four quadrants of BooFaye's body cut—two front and two back (see figure 12A, 12B, 12C, and 12D).

2. BooFaye's arms can be made from any rectangular shape that is at least 5 inches (12.7 cm) wide. Use the top edge of one of BooFaye's arm rectangles to measure the width of the pieces you'll cut for her spiky fingers. Align the arm rectangle atop two pieces of lining or fabric of your choice. Trace the top edge of the arm, and using that line as a bottom edge, cut triangular forms of the size and shape you want the finger spikes to be (see figures 12E and 12F).

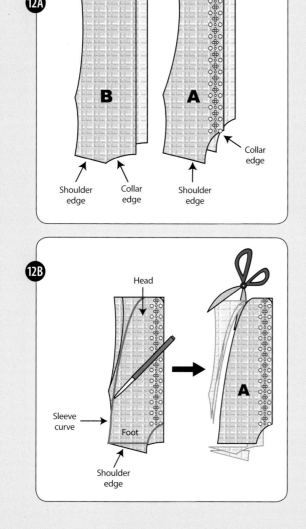

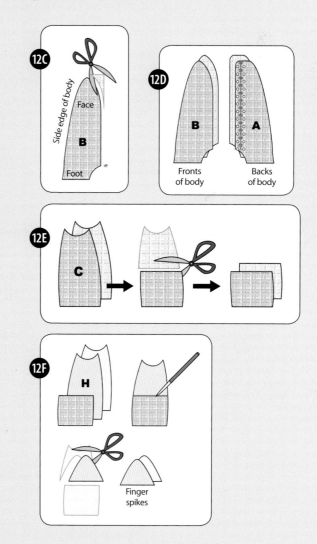

3. Cut out six toenail shapes from a piece of lining to appliqué onto BooFaye's feet. Cut out a big lippy shape to plaster onto her face. Cut a circle for BooFaye's eye from any fabric you choose (see figures 12G and 12H).

4. Create circles for BooFaye's feet using the Creature Feature Bottoms instructions on page 28 for tips on how to do this (see figure 12I).

5. Use the two layers of the jacket's collar and the sleeve cuffs as they are for BooFaye's spinal ridges and ears (see figure 12J). If you've followed the projects in this book in sequence, you'll have done two sets of spinal ridges already (see Gilmor Oothby on page 62 and Camilla Grace on page 80). If this is your first time making spinal ridges, then read on.

Now observe figure 12K to see the inventory of parts we've cut for BooFaye. She will nix you from the next party invitation list if you've let a piece go missing.

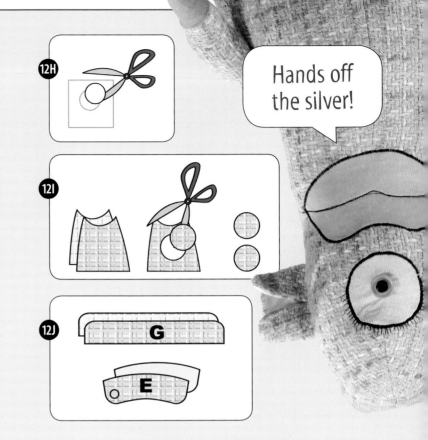

Hands off the silver!

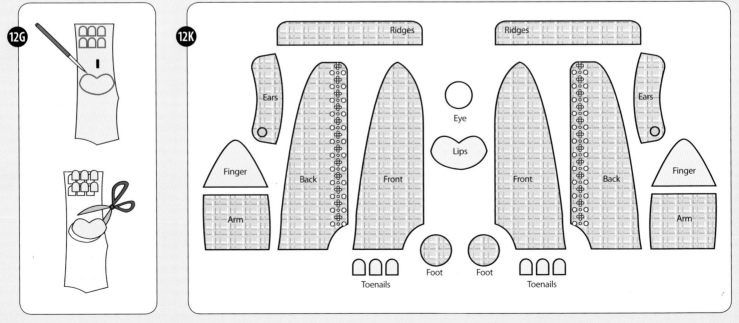

Stitching

6. To make BooFaye's spinal ridges, take both parts G and align them together with right sides touching. Lay them on a piece of padding or batting that's cut to size.

Draw a series of ridges along part F. Stitch along the line you drew and trim around your seam leaving ³/₈-inch (.95 cm) seam allowance. Don't forget to notch the corners in between the ridges.

Turn the ridges right side out, trapping the padding layer in between the fabric. Stitch a seam ¹/₄ to ³/₈ inch (.64 to .95 cm) away from the edge to stabilize the piece (see figure 12L).

7. Insert the ridges—points first—between the spine edges of BooFaye's back parts. Match the open edge of her ridges with the spine edges, and stitch those edges shut, fixing the ridges into place (see figure 12M).

8. Align the parts you cut for BooFaye's front with right sides touching. Stitch the parts together down the straight edge (see figure 12N).

9. Now that BooFaye's front is stitched up, appliqué her eye, lips, and toenails in place. Stitch a line across the lips to define where they part, and give her a disapproving grimace (see figure 12O).

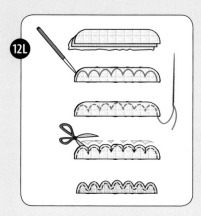

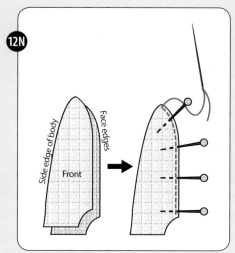

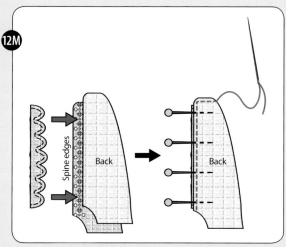

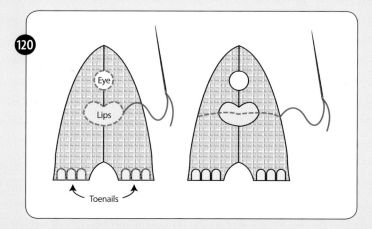

10. Grab one of the arm rectangles and one of the shapes you cut for her finger spikes. Align the shapes right sides together and matching their edges. Stitch them together. Fold the stitched arm in half vertically with right sides touching. Pin the arm at the seams, and stitch down the long edge. Stuff the arm, and leave ½ inch (1.3 cm) of space unstuffed at the open end (see figures 12P and 12Q). Now, make another one!

11. Use the sleeve cuffs to make the ears. Fold them in a loop so that their ends meet in the middle. That's all you need to do. Sandwich BooFaye's ears and arms between the front and back of her body wherever you think they should go. Match the open edges of the ears and arms to the side edges of BooFaye's body. Pin the whole sandwich together and stitch around the outside edges of BooFaye's body leaving ⅜-inch (1.3 cm) seam allowance. Leave the bottoms of her feet and a small space between her legs unstitched (see figures 12R and 12S).

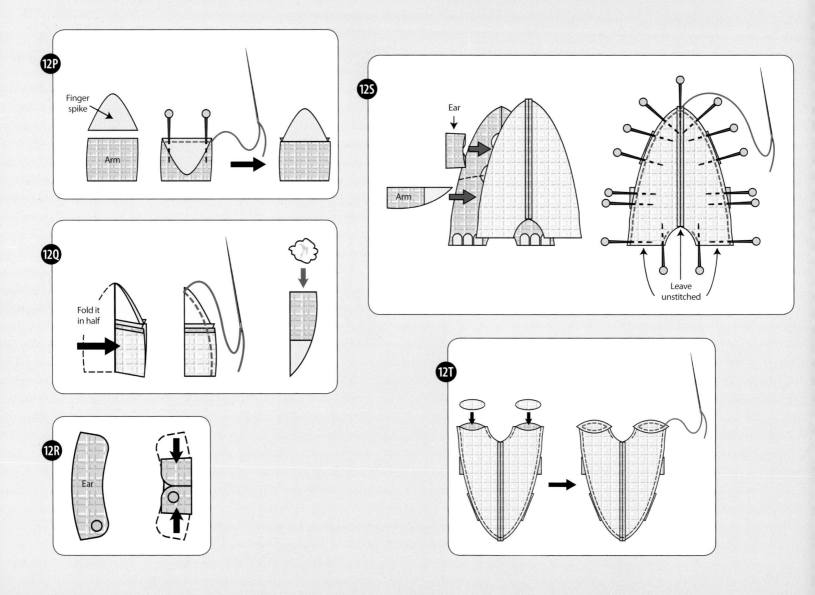

12. Follow the Creature Feature Bottoms instructions on page 28 to attach foot bottoms to the open edges of her legs (see figure 12T).

13. Turn BooFaye right side out, and stuff her through the unstitched space you left in step 11 (see figure 12U). Close her up using the closing stitch found on page 16. Finish BooFaye off with a nice button sewn onto her eye. Find a bejeweled one if you can, because in her mind, she's on a parade float.

Don't wait around to find a pearl inlaid pink tweed jacket before making your own BooFaye. You don't even need to find a jacket. Trouser legs or long sleeves can provide the shapes you need for the four quarters of BooFaye's body. The rest is up to your imagination.

I may be a lady, but my fingers are perfect for pointing.

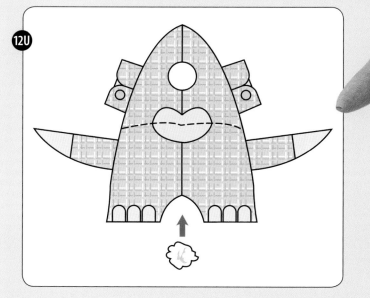

12U

Precious Mumpkins

We all need a nice, subservient pet to yap at our toes while we try to cook. It doesn't need to be smart, just passably cute, and constantly underfoot. Precious Mumpkins is my answer to that need. Even if you (accidentally, of course) bash Precious Mumpkins in the face with a hot frying pan, he'll still lick up the grease and love you all the same.

{ *When I saw this dress, I couldn't place its vintage—the 60s or perhaps the 23rd century? And who wore it—a stylish European air hostess, a secretary in the typing pool, or a starship captain? The structure of the fantastic armholes looked like open, eager mouths begging for treats, so that's what inspired this monster.* }

You probably won't find this dress just anywhere (if you do, please let me know). So few dresses, in my limited experience, are made with such stylishly-shaped panels. Think of this project as boldly going where no one has gone before. We'll forget the Disassembly Chart and just start hacking into this rare find. But do look at the diagram of the dress provided.

Ack...I just swallowed a moth!

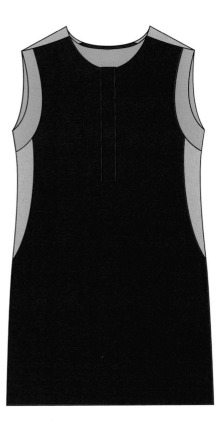

1. Think of the armhole as Mumpkins' mouth. Think of the shoulder of the dress as the top of Mumpkins' head. Draw a line on the dress for Mumpkins' back and the bottom of his body. Cut along the line you drew, slicing through both layers of the dress (see figure 13A).

2. Use your fashion ruler or a flexible tape measure to measure Mumpkins' back. Use that measurement to create a wedge for Mumpkins' back. Cut the wedge from the back of the dress, or wherever there's plenty of fabric (see figure 13B).

3. Let's make Mumpkins' ears with the other armhole. Or, you can cut whatever ear shapes you want from anywhere you please on the dress (see figure 13C).

13A

Shoulder

Arm hole

Mumkins' back

Bottom of body

13B

Measure Mumkins' back

13C

Sleeve edges

Sleeve

4. You'll need to make some lining for the ears. Lay the ears atop some contrasting fabric with right sides touching. Trace the ears and cut the shapes out along the lines you drew (see figure 13D).

5. Use dark or black fabric to cut an oval for the interior of Mumpkins' mouth. The oval should be 2 inches (5 cm) or so larger in length and width than the opening of the mouth. Use a contrasting or light-colored fabric to cut a tongue to appliqué onto Mumpkins' mouth (see figure 13E).

6. Choose some fabric to cut out eyes and enough parts for the eight (or more!) teeth you want Mumpkins to have (see figure 13F).

And for our relatively short list of Mumpkins parts, please have a look at figure 13G. And remember to let me know if you found this exact dress!

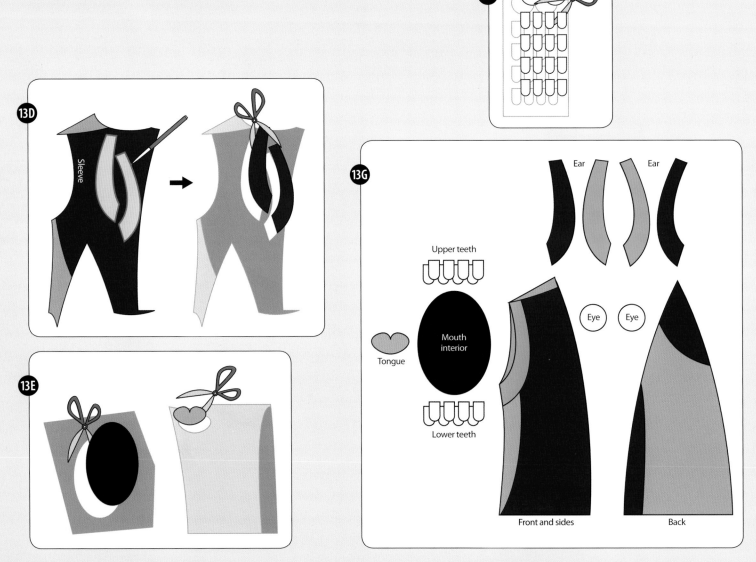

13D

Sleeve

13F

13G

Ear   Ear

Upper teeth

Tongue   Mouth interior   Eye   Eye

Lower teeth

13E

Front and sides   Back

Stitching

7. Review the appliqué instructions on page 33, and then stitch the tongue onto his mouth interior and the eyes alongside his mouth (see figures 13H and 13I).

8. Flatten Mumpkins as best you can with his wrong side up. Arrange his teeth around the edge of his mouth where you think they ought to go. Make sure the open edges of the teeth face away from the mouth opening. Align Mumpkins' mouth interior atop the teeth with the tongue side down. Make sure the edges of the teeth are visible at the edge of the mouth interior. Pin the mouth into place, sandwiching all the teeth. Make sure the mouth opening is completely covered by the mouth interior. Stitch around the edge of the mouth (see figure 13J).

9. Follow the Serendipitous Ear instructions on page 25 to make Mumpkins' ears. With the wrong side of the body front facing up, place the ears on the body where you think they ought to go. Align the edges of the wedge you cut for the back of Mumpkins' body to the edges of the front and sides of his body. Pin everything together securely and stitch around the edges leaving 3/8-inch (.95 cm) seam allowance. Leave about 4 inches (10 cm) unstitched down the middle of one of the edges for turning and stuffing (see figures 13K and 13L).

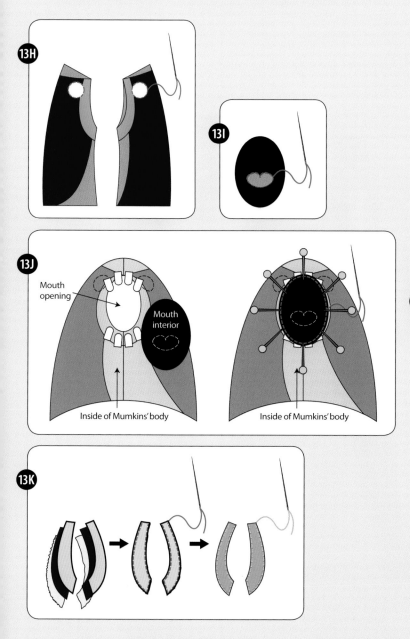

13H

13I

13J

Mouth opening

Mouth interior

Inside of Mumkins' body

Inside of Mumkins' body

13K

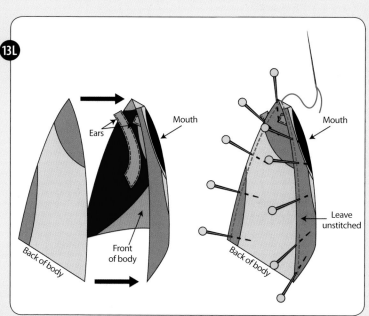

13L

Ears

Mouth

Mouth

Back of body

Front of body

Back of body

Leave unstitched

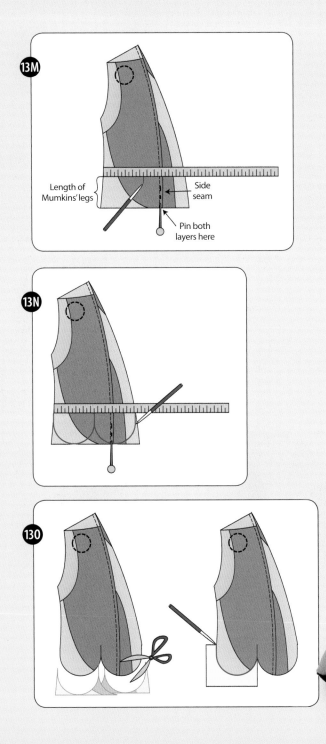

13M
Length of Mumkins' legs
Side seam
Pin both layers here

13N

13O

10. Keep Mumpkins' body wrong side out and lay him flat to one side. Pin both layers together at the side seam so that the body aligns perfectly. Decide how long you want Mumpkins' legs to be and lay a ruler that distance away from the bottom edge. Mark the midpoint on Mumpkins' body where you've laid the ruler. Draw two identical, even, rounded legs that extend from the ruler to the bottom edge of Mumpkins' body. You may use a compass if you want (see figures 13M and 13N).

A gnat done flew down my throat!

11. Cut out the legs along the line you drew, and trace one of the legs onto a piece of sturdy paper. Cut out the leg template you traced, and trace it again four times onto sturdy paper, making kind of a four-leaf clover with your pattern. Cut the shape out (see figures 13O and 13P).

12. Trace the template you made onto a large portion of remaining fabric from the dress. Cut the shape out (see figure 13Q).

13. Keep Mumpkins' body wrong side out. Align the leg bottoms (wrong side out) with the edges of the legs on Mumpkins' body. Pin the edges of the body and the leg bottoms together, matching curves and corners. Stitch around all the edges leaving ⅜-inch (.95 cm) seam allowance. Don't forget to notch the corners between all of Mumpkins' legs (see figure 13R).

14. Turn Precious Mumpkins right side out through the hole you left in his back. Stuff him as firmly as you'd like.

Finish Mumpkins off by stitching buttons onto his big, bewildered eyes. And there you go. Congratulate yourself for working your way through 13 plush toy clothing challenges. You're a fashion UN-designer.

Sundresses, muscle shirts, and other sleeveless garments can be used to make a Precious Mumpkins. Heck, even long-sleeved items could give you a long snouted monster. As with any of these patterns, once you learn a technique, you can apply it almost anywhere. You're obviously an intelligent person: Find the monster within and let him (or her) out!

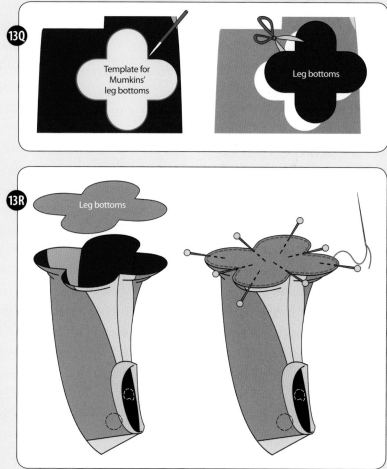

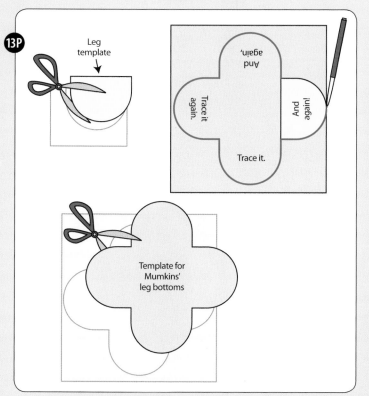

About the Author

John Murphy is the author of *Stupid Sock Creatures* (Lark Crafts, 2005) and has co-written several other plush works including *Plush-O-Rama* by Linda Kopp (Lark Crafts, 2006) and *Invasion of the Plush Monsters* by Veronika Gunter (featuring Ian Dennis and Jenny Harada) (Lark Crafts, 2008).

His work has appeared in other books such as *Green Design* (Mark Batty Publisher), *Art Doll Adventures* by Li Hertzi (Quarry Books), and *Dot Dot Dash* (Gestalten). Most recently, he has collaborated with illustrator Liana Finck to create *Revelations and the Stupid Creatures* (Mark Batty Publisher), an adaptation of the last book of the Bible, as told by plush creatures. It will be available in 2010. John has also appeared on an episode of HGTV's *That's Clever* and on Threadbanger.com (Next New Networks).

After seven short years in the DIY plush world, John has decided to take a break from the full-time rigors of running an art studio to pursue another line of work for which he feels just as much passion. He will begin work as a teacher and counselor at a wilderness camp for at-risk teenagers. John will remain available over email and snail mail for questions and answers about any of his books. Feel free to send word to John if you need him to come give a lesson.

Find all of John's contact information and follow his adventures at www.stupidcreatures.com.

Acknowledgments

My thanks for encouragement, friendship, and help throughout the writing process go to my parents, siblings, and friends. Special thanks go to the Cooks and Matt Parris for their generosity and hospitality. My thanks also go to Tyler Dockery and Chris Knotts for a humor assist. To the Jobes, the Krauses, Carmen from En-Zed, and everyone else I've come to know because of the Sock Creatures, thank you for an incredible journey.

Can someone take me home? I forgot my pills.

I don't know what all this blathering is about. We're the real stars.

Index

Appliqué, 33

Arms, 18–20
  Freefingers, 20
  Gusseted palms, 18–19

Attaching,
  Arc Method, 30–31
  Bubble Method, 32–33
  Circumference Method, 31
  Tuck and Sew Method, 30

Bottoms, 28–29

Creatures made from
  Dress/curtainy things, 102, 134
  Jackets, 44, 110, 126
  Pajamas, 80
  Pants, 52, 88, 118
  Shirts, 36, 72
  Suits, 96
  Sweaters, 62, 71

Disassembly, 13–14

Ears and Horns, 25–26
  A Horn of Your Own, 26
  As-Is, 26
  Mentacle, 26
  Serendipitous Ear, 25

Eyes, 28

Fabric types, 9–10

Legs, 21–24
  Add-a-Stub, 24
  Basic dangly legs, 21
  Dangly leg with toe, 22
  Stub, 23

Notching, 16–17

Oval bottoms, 29

Seam allowance, 15

Stitching, 15–16

Stuffing, 17

Supplies, 11–12

Teeth, 27

Tongues, 27–28

Top-stitching, 33

There are others?!?

Can't get enough monsters? **Try these creatures!**

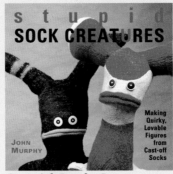

Plush-o-Rama
Curious Creatures for
Immature Adults
ISBN 9781600590177

Just take fabric, a needle and
thread, and stuffing, combine a
touch of cuteness with a dash
of utter weirdness, and you've
got some of the oddest, most
irresistible creatures ever. These
30+ projects are unabashedly
handmade, but bold, colorful,
and totally loveable.

Invasion of the
Plush Monsters!
Wickedly Weird Creatures
You Just Gotta Sew
ISBN 9781579909437

They're frighteningly adorable,
and they're about to conquer
the world! Kids will enjoy
getting in on the crafting fun
with a dozen simple, cute,
odd, and irresistible projects:
creatures sporting Velcro faces
(change expressions everyday!)
or serving double duty as
cozies, backpacks, and pillows.

Stupid Sock Creatures
Making Quirky, Lovable Figures
from Cast-off Socks
ISBN 9781579906108

Possessed of irresistible
charm, this book offers all
the inspiration you need to
transform cast-off socks into
wickedly funny toys. There's
Claude with his perplexed
expression and tiny tail that
stands at full attention; Jorden,
always on the prowl with his
three eyes; and a host of other
fun personalities to create.

Make Your Own
Stupid Sock Creatures
ISBN 9781600594403

Can't find socks to transform?
Use some of ours! With snazzy
striped socks, a pair of solid
anklets, and some stuffing,
you can get right to stitching.
In addition to the supplies,
you'll also get a 48-page
instructional booklet, plus
a super cool design for a
rainbow-striped creature!